LIFE AS THE NOTRE DAME LEPRECHAUN

Behind the Face of the Fighting Irish

To Dave-

Stay Golden!

To Dave -

Stay Golden!

LIFE AS THE NOTRE DAME LEPRECHAUN

Behind the Face of the Fighting Irish

DANIEL COLT COLLINS

LIFE AS THE NOTRE DAME LEPRECHAUN:
Behind the Face of the Fighting Irish

10 9 8 7 6 5 4 3 2

ISBN: 978-0-9890731-5-8

Distributed by ACTA Publications
4848 N. Clark Street, Chicago, IL 60640.
800-397-2282
www.actapublications.com

Published by
CORBY BOOKS
A Division of Corby Publishing, LP
P.O. Box 93
Notre Dame, IN 46556
Editorial Office: (574) 784-3482

Manufactured in the United States of America

Contents

Dedication

To my mom, whose unceasing selfless love stands behind every story in this book. Thank you for inspiring me to keep looking up towards the sky.

To my dad, the best fan a Leprechaun could ever ask for. Thank you for your humble grace and your perspective on life, both of which have taught me more than words on a page could ever convey.

To Fr. George Rozum. Thank you for turning generations of Dawgs into Blessed Men and Brothers.

To my family, friends, teachers, Domers, Dawgs, and all those who use their talents to do God's work. The inspiration you generate changes lives every day. Keep it up.

To Notre Dame, my beloved Alma Mater. Stay Golden.

September 5, 2009

#23 Notre Dame Fighting Irish
vs.
Nevada Wolf Pack

Notre Dame Stadium
Notre Dame, IN

BLOOD RUSHED TO MY HEAD. My vision blurred. The blazing Midwest summer sun beat down on the back of my neck. Beads of sweat gathered where my bowler hat met my brow, dripping in endless rows down my nose. I wiped my sweaty palms against my bright green knickers one at a time so I could readjust my grip on the slippery steel of the giant flagpole I held in my hands. Over 81,000 voices hushed in the ninety-degree heat, waiting to erupt on my cue. I could feel the weight of over 162,000 eyes bearing down on me. Only one thought filled my mind: "Don't trip!"

An entire herd of raging bulls in golden helmets filled the tunnel behind me, penned in by only a few coaches attempting to keep them at bay as they began to sway back and forth in nervous excitement. They personified the mounting anticipation that had built up all off-season. The entire stadium filled to the brim with an electric charge.

I didn't even have time to think how crazy it was that all these people expected me to lead this team of super humans out onto the field when suddenly the familiar voice of Mike Collins blared over the loudspeakers: "Heeeeeeeere come the Irish!" Mike wasn't lying. The Irish were coming right at me.

A flash of gold hit my eye as they burst out of the tunnel into the sunlight, and I was off to the races. The explosion of the crowd came with far more force than I could have anticipated, nearly knocking me off my feet. I suddenly remembered my mantra, repeating, "Don't trip! Don't trip! Don't trip!" over and over in my head as I ran.

A tidal wave of energy swept me up as my feet barely grazed the ground for the entire 100-yard sprint down the field. Once I made it to the far end zone I triumphantly waved the Blue and Gold to our sellout crowd and millions more watching on TV. As my adrenaline subsided and exhaustion set in, a new thought filled my head: "This is what living feels like." An inescapable smile spread across my face while I paused to take it all in.

A wildly unlikely journey had brought me to this unforgettable moment in my life, and an even more unbelievable story was about to unfold.

Chapter I

An Unlikely Journey

I MAY NOT HAVE GROWN UP a Notre Dame fan, but I was born to wear that green suit.

Lou Holtz won a national championship with the Fighting Irish in 1988, the same year I was born. Although the course of my childhood in Hamburg, New York, a southern suburb of Buffalo, led nowhere even remotely near that Catholic university in Northern Indiana, I had heard of it. Still, Notre Dame seemed to be the furthest thing from my mind as a kid.

I never developed much of an interest in watching professional sports since I was too young to remember the glory days of the Buffalo Bills and Sabres. At over two hours away, Syracuse was the closest college with even a mediocre sports program, but I always hated the color orange. Yet, despite such beginnings, an odd combination of fate, lucky breaks and blessings eventually led me to become the face of one of the largest and most devoted fan bases in the world.

Completely unbeknownst to me, several strange coincidences planted the seeds early on in life for my future as a Leprechaun. My best friend Drew was already obsessed with Notre Dame by the time we reached grade school—and so was the rest of his family, led by his older cousin Mitch who was, and still is, downright fanatical. I couldn't understand how a whole family could care so much about the Fighting Irish just because they had Irish blood running through their veins, but they really did bleed blue and gold.

It always seemed weird to me that my best friend was so invested in a random school he had never even been to, but I looked up to him and he made it cool. He wanted to be in their marching band because he was first-chair trombone and he liked their blue and gold slide covers. He decked out his bedroom with Fighting Irish gear, complete with a sheet set, pictures on every wall, and even a garbage can with a big interlocking "ND" on the side. I filled my bedroom with G.I. Joes and Star Wars action figures.

Drew had a small stuffed toy in the shape of a Leprechaun that would yell, "Go Irish!" when someone hit it, and then play the beginning of the Notre Dame Victory March when someone hit it again. We used to run around his house whipping that thing at each other as hard as we could. I took a good "Go Irish!" to the face on more than one occasion.

According to Drew's grandfather, whom we called "Poppy," I was all but predestined to become a Leprechaun. A hilariously sarcastic Irishman with a heart of gold, Poppy made fun of me relentlessly about pretty much everything, but mostly about my small stature. He would look me in the eye and tell me that anyone who said I could be anything I wanted to be in life was feeding me pure bullshit. Nope, as Poppy saw it I had only two choices in life. I could become either a professional jockey or the Notre Dame Leprechaun. Poppy habitually grilled me about far more pressing matters than being small, so I never paid much attention to his prophecy until I found myself choosing the latter path much later in life. I sometimes wonder how everything would have turned out if instead I had taken my middle name literally and chosen to ride ponies for a living.

The single most lasting influence that forever changed the way I looked at sports took place while I attended Hamburg Middle School. My friends and I started going to Hamburg High School football games every Saturday afternoon, mainly to watch the cheerleaders and buy cheap candy from the snack shack. That's when I first came across Jimmy Ryan. Hamburg had a horrible football team, but Jimmy wore a purple and white tuxedo to every home game, where he proceeded to steal the show week in and week out. He led the entire student section in the most ridiculous chants anyone had ever heard, he fired off ingenious insults at opposing fans, and he got the whole crowd roaring with laughter by pretending to teach the cheerleaders how to do pushups. He was way cooler than Hamburg's lame foam-headed bulldog mascot, and I remember sitting on those rickety wooden bleachers in awe of the power he had over the crowd. Not only that, but he harnessed the collective energy of the masses to generate an even greater power. He acted like he was completely free and impervious to all embarrassment, all while having the time of his life. Simply put, he was the man. I would always remember that; and years later, whenever I stepped onto the field as the Notre Dame Leprechaun, I made a conscious effort to channel my inner Jimmy Ryan.

After middle school I had the good fortune of attending Nichols School, the best and brightest private high school in Buffalo. Nichols offered so much on so many levels, but the lack of school spirit I found there shocked me. I put up with it for a while, until one day I decided to take matters into my own hands. My best friend Dan and I had nothing to do one day after school, so on a whim we geared up for a girls' basketball game. We went out and bought bright green t-shirts, green and white checkered pajama pants, huge green wigs, and lime green face paint. Running into the gym just before tip-off, we went completely bonkers for about an hour straight. Our antics weren't quite as refined as Jimmy Ryan's just yet, but we caught the attention of both teams on the court, the scattered gathering of parents in attendance, and even a local news station, which featured us for about half a second during their local sports special that night. I was hooked.

The very next day I recruited my best friend Mike to help me take this whole school spirit thing to the next level by founding the highly sophisticated association we dubbed the Nichols Spirit Club. First, we drafted a mission statement and held our inaugural board meeting. Next, we got to work mass-producing customized t-shirts for our members and planning a series of morning announcements to notify the entire school of our presence. In almost no time at all, we found ourselves at the helm of the largest student organization at Nichols, ready to revive school spirit where previously none had existed.

Mike and I led the charge when it came to acting as obnoxiously as we could while also maintaining the sense of class expected of well-polished Nichols students. We strove to provide our school with as much of a home-field advantage as possible, and we even travelled far and wide to our opponents' venues. Our ardent zeal for the Nichols Big Green soon became contagious, and we had fun watching it spread. I loved competing for Nichols in football and lacrosse, but my best high school memories involved supporting my classmates from the stands, creating a source of positive energy that grew far beyond what I could have produced alone, while not taking myself too seriously in the process.

Not only did Nichols Football teach me how to lose with grace, but it also sent me to Notre Dame. No, my tremendous upside as a 5′6″, 140-lb., every-down running back didn't land me a scholarship offer from the Fighting Irish. Instead, it got me watching football on TV almost constantly. We played our games on Saturdays, so I was never able to watch very much live college football action. Luckily for me, I got suspended for the season finale of my senior year (following an ejection from the previous game for taunting opposing fans—I really couldn't help myself). That bummed me out, but it also cleared up my schedule for watching more college football.

When Saturday came I hugged my football, flopped down on the couch, and flipped on the TV. The NBC Peacock appeared on the screen and I watched as a student section, motioned and chanted in unison. It looked like fun. Next came a montage of tailgates, parades, touch football, crunchy leaves, bagpipes, and barbecues spread all across a beautifully traditional-looking campus on a perfectly crisp autumn afternoon. It looked really fun. A voice cheerfully exclaimed, "We'll be back with more Notre Dame Football after these messages!"

Without lifting my head from the pillow I yelled out across my house, "Hey, mom! I think I'll apply to Notre Dame!"

"But we don't even know anything about it! Where is it?"

"I don't know. I think it's in Indiana. It looks sweet, though!"

"What about the nine other schools we actually visited?"

"If I get into Notre Dame, we can go see it then."

"Um...okay...if you say so."

And so it began. I applied to Notre Dame even though I knew next to nothing about it other than what I remembered from Drew's childhood obsession and the ten seconds I had just witnessed on NBC. Soon after, I went to hear a Notre Dame admissions recruiter speak at a nearby Catholic high school. He seemed authentically friendly as he welcomed us, gave us a rundown of the admissions process, and warned us against comparing ourselves to Rudy in our application essays. Once that "Here Come the Irish" music video finished flashing across the screen of his portable projector, I felt ready to run through a brick wall for the Fighting Irish. If that soul-piercing voice, coupled with grainy images of old-timey football players, a priest walking across campus in slow motion, drums, bagpipes, and more kids playing touch football in crunchy leaves could send chills up my spine like that, I could only imagine what would happen if I got in and actually visited the place.

The mail truck came just as I finished shoveling my Jeep out of the snow. I momentarily delayed the lunch date I had with my mom at J.P. Fitzgerald's, my favorite McIrish Pub, by running out to the mailbox. There it was. Notre Dame sent me the big package. My mom's response to the acceptance letter went something like this: "Holy shit!" My next words: "I guess we get to find out where this place is now."

Eight hours of driving came to an end when we took a left from Angela Boulevard onto Notre Dame Avenue in the middle of a freezing rainstorm. Even against such a miserable backdrop, the Golden Dome looked immaculate. We toured campus amidst giant raindrops hurled sideways by gale-force winds, and we felt sorry for our tour guide as he trudged bravely across campus just to make sure one single prospective student had a good experience. I never forgot that first example of the way Notre Dame students take such pride in contributing to the spirit of their school, no matter how small their contributions may seem at the time. His simple gesture changed my life, and I am forever grateful.

After our tour I ventured out on my own towards O'Neil Hall to meet my student hosts for the evening. The group of freshmen I stayed with welcomed me graciously from the very beginning by taking several hours out of their busy work schedules to show me a good time on a slow Tuesday. Not only did they introduce me to the magnificent sport of beer pong, but they even included me on their late-night run to Reckers, the 24-hour café on campus, where I ate cheese fries and attempted in vain to convince a group of sophomore girls that I had seen them before in class. My host stayed up with me until two in the morning—talking, laughing, and listing all the ways his school was most definitely cooler than my previous top choice, Georgetown. In the morning I accompanied him to what would end up being the only math class I ever attended at Notre Dame. I followed him out of the clasroom feeling exhausted but exhilarated. I liked college, especially this one. When my mom picked me up, she could tell right away by the look on my face. The next time we turned from Angela Boulevard onto Notre Dame Avenue, I would be a Domer.

Chapter II

Freshman Year: Welcome to the Dawg House

THE DEEP ECHO OF DRUMS sounded from somewhere down below, gradually growing in strength until the brass blast of trumpets exploded out into the arena. Most of the incoming freshmen had already assembled with their families inside the Joyce Center, and everyone stood simultaneously as if literally pulled up out of their seats by the first notes of the fight song. I looked around as everyone clapped along in unison, half expecting to see thunder actually shaking down from the sky. Out of nowhere a fiery redhead in a blazing green suit appeared onstage with a hearty "Let's go, all you Aaaaah-rish!"

All eyes focused on Leprechaun Kevin as he hopped and skipped about, noticeably having the time of his life. I thought about how much fun his job must be, and I pictured myself up there welcoming freshmen to campus one day. He told us that we had a lot to look forward to during freshman orientation, and he made every mom in attendance cry when he said that he considered us all part of his Notre Dame family now. I became teary-eyed myself for the first of many times on campus when we learned how to link arms and sway while singing the Alma Mater.

From the first moment I stepped onto campus as a freshman, I felt lucky to be part of this whole Notre Dame thing. I had walked into a world like none other, full of extraordinary people working with confident devotion in profound ways to accomplish even more profound goals. On top of that, every student I met had either won a high school state championship in their favorite sport or some sort of award for helping little old ladies cross streets while at the same time rescuing their cats from trees. I would have been overwhelmed by it all if everyone hadn't been so damn nice, but everywhere I turned a smiling face greeted me with enthusiastic kindness.

The Blessed Men and Brothers of Alumni Hall had sent me a packet over the summer to fill me in on the essentials of my new home. They called themselves "the Dawgs," they pledged allegiance to a legendary man they called FGR, they wore green and white, they had the only set of Greek letters on campus and, by the looks of it, they liked to party. They also listed "The Center of the Universe" as their location since Alumni Hall stands proudly alongside Main Circle at the head of Notre Dame Avenue.

Upon arriving at the center of the universe, I discovered that I would be living alongside fifteen other freshmen in a hallway affectionately known as "Shit Alley" due to its closet-like rooms and its proximity to the malodorous garbage chutes. The initial shock at my first glimpse of my soon-to-be living conditions quickly dissipated though, as one by one I began to meet the colorful cast of characters who would eventually become my brothers for life—Joey, Paul, Kevin, Vu, Chris, Chris, Matt, Robbie, Drew, Vince, Michael, Trey, Rob, Bert, Goody, and I bonded out of necessity. Our tight living quarters brought us together, literally, and we developed a sense of Shit Alley solidarity from the very beginning.

☘

At the conclusion of the weekend-long pseudo speed-dating session known as freshman orientation, the sophomores who had been named to the Alumni Hall frosh-o committee called all of us freshmen together into the basement rec room. With an air of gravity they told us how FGR, the beloved priest serving as our rector, had caught wind of several freshmen sneaking alcohol to frosh-o events. This left FGR feeling deeply disappointed, and he wanted to pay each of us a visit starting at midnight. The sophomores told us to go wait patiently in our rooms.

At the stroke of midnight Alumni Hall came alive with reverberations of intense shouting and vigorous pounding on wooden doors. The sophomores ran down each and every hallway, telling the freshmen to gear up for a run. I had no idea what to expect, but I sensed something unforgettable unfolding. Hurriedly lacing up my running shoes as I hopped out the door, I made it to Main Circle just in time to join the fifty or so freshmen already pumping out pushups. The sophomores walked through our ranks like drill sergeants, telling us to embrace the glorious pain because tonight we would earn the right to call ourselves Dawgs. Then, as soon as we reached a sufficient level of fatigue, they instructed us to follow as they took off running.

Our "Dawg Run" turned into more of a marathon than a sprint as we crisscrossed campus several times on our way to each women's dorm, where we serenaded our female classmates with Celine Dion's "My Heart Will Go On"—better known in Alumni Hall as "The Deal Sealer." As I began to tire, I noticed more and more sophomores urging freshmen onward with helping hands, kind patience, and words of encouragement. They made sure we never left a fellow Dawg behind and, despite the whole drill sergeant act they put on, I could tell they really cared.

With all of us just about ready to collapse, we reached the last stop on our run and basked in our collective sense of accomplishment while bathing in the rejuvenating waters of Stonehenge Fountain. We had earned it, and we could now count ourselves among the Blessed Men and Brothers of Alumni Hall. A celebration of brotherly love ensued on the steps of the Golden Dome, where most of us smoked our first victory cigars.

Everyone on campus quickly turned their attention to football as the 2006 season drew near for Charlie Weis's

Fighting Irish, who boasted a #3 preseason ranking on the eve of Brady Quinn's senior year. The echoes seemed fully awake, and syllabus week flew by as if time itself couldn't wait for our first game. Saturday night came, and we all watched the live broadcast of our season opener at Georgia Tech on a giant screen in the middle of North Quad. We barely squeaked by the unranked Yellow Jackets by only four points and our ranking fell to #5, but the hype surrounding our home opener against #19 Penn State took almost no time to spiral out of control. I heard rumors of students selling tickets for over a thousand dollars a pop, but I never once entertained such a thought.

I couldn't have dreamt up a better scenario for my first game inside Notre Dame Stadium. Game day brought with it the perfect combination of pregame partying, classic college football pageantry, and an added pinch of importance to make the impending showdown even more flavorful. Upon entering "the house that Rockne built," I immediately identified with Rudy's dad when he said, "This is the most beautiful sight these eyes have ever seen." His phrase became my recurring thought throughout the game as our student section detonated with every Fighting Irish touchdown en route to a 41-17 massacre of the Nittany Lions. I hadn't seen so many pushups since the Dawg Run two weeks earlier, and there was Leprechaun Kevin beaming with pride in the middle of it all.

I called my mom pretty much constantly during the first few weeks of school, so she already knew how thrilled I felt about joining such an inspiring new community. She put it best in the letter she sent me following my first football weekend at Notre Dame:

> Dear Dan,
>
> When the football team and cheerleaders came running out onto the field my eyes filled up with tears because I was so happy that my son was part of such a wonderful day. I watched every moment of the game and all I kept thinking was: "This is why Dan worked so hard for all these years." This is your reward: not only the education, but the complete and total joy of celebrating a new spirit and a new sense of camaraderie. Not many will ever experience anything like this. Notre Dame is where you belong, and it will always be yours.
>
> Love, Mom

Life was good and I bragged to my friends back home about our shiny new #2 ranking—until our third game ended in a devastating 47-21 loss to the rotten, putrid, stinking Skunkbears of Michigan. At that point our ranking fell to #13. Then we almost blew the entire season during our fourth game as we found ourselves down by 10 to Michigan State with less than eight minutes remaining. Luckily, Brady Quinn's composure in the stinging rain of East Lansing showed all of us freshmen what it meant to be as cool as a cucumber, and Terrail Lambert's pair of interceptions in the final minutes taught us not to ever give up on the Fighting Irish. Those of us watching the miracle win from the warm comforts of our dorms decided to celebrate by voluntarily getting as cold and wet as our beloved team. I slipped and gashed my knee on the slippery marble of Stonehenge Fountain as I joined thousands of my classmates in an epic Irish jig, actually feeling kind of honored that my blood became part of those sacred waters. In just my first month of college I had already enjoyed two separate moments of pure bliss in that fountain.

By the time we hosted UCLA during week seven, our ranking had climbed back to #8, only to fall into jeopardy once again due to a heart-attack-inducing near upset. When Jeff Samardzija caught a last-chance prayer from Brady Quinn, turned it upfield, juked a defender, and sealed our victory with a ballerina-esque plié into the end zone, row 37 of section 31 jumped all at once with such force that we cracked our wooden bench in half right down the middle. I took a few splinters home as souvenirs.

My first taste of a stadium-wide "Beat SC" chant gave me goose bumps after we crushed unranked Army 41-9 on senior day, but unfortunately the #6 Fighting Irish couldn't hang with the #2 Trojans the following week. They ruined my Thanksgiving to the tune of a 44-24 beat down. Then we ended up piling on another loss to finish out our season with a 10-3 record after losing to #4 LSU 41-14 in the Sugar Bowl. My trip to New Orleans wasn't a complete loss, though. I had the pleasure of becoming cordially acquainted with several charming, camouflage-wearing, confederate-flag-waving, middle-finger-wagging, "Tiger Bait"-chanting LSU fans. As hard as they tried, their taunts couldn't faze me. After all, I knew I would witness at least one bowl victory at some point during the three years I had left on my magic-carpet ride as a Notre Dame student.

☘

The magic of my first semester carried over into the next, culminating in another matchup between Notre Dame and an SEC powerhouse ranked #4 in the nation. This time, the unranked Fighting Irish hosted the heavily favored Alabama Crimson Tide for a prime-time showdown on ESPN's Friday night college basketball showcase. Once our classes let out for the week, we decided to join the upperclassmen who invited us to partake in their time-honored tradition of "40s at 4." After finishing a 40 oz. bottle of my namesake Colt .45, I felt confident that I had accrued enough liquid courage for our entire basketball team. For some reason, this convinced me that we would win the game and everyone would get to storm the court. None of my friends took my prediction too seriously.

We all found ourselves in a rare state as our Fighting Irish began to pull away from the Crimson Tide late in the second half. At one point Leprechaun Kevin threw a souvenir t-shirt directly at me, so I stood on the back of my seat to up my chances of outreaching my much taller friends. Just as the rolled-up shirt hit my outstretched fingertips, my good friend Carl speared me in the back and we tumbled over the row of girls in front of us, laughing too hard to get up. Coach Brey called a timeout with just a few minutes left, and I told the young ladies that I looked forward to seeing them again very soon at center court. I never quite made it that far as double zeros filled the clock and I found myself nearly trampled to death by a frenzied mob. In a last-ditch effort to avoid my certain demise, I called out for my fellow Dawg John Ryan to save me. Lucky for me, John played defensive end on the football team. I enjoyed the view from his shoulders as I floated atop the green sea of swaying students, praying that my recurring dream of surreal Alma Mater moments would continue.

☘

After enduring a semester and a half of friends and strangers telling me that I should try out to become the next Notre Dame Leprechaun every time my Nichols Spirit Club mentality resurfaced at a home game, I finally mustered up enough courage to approach Leprechaun Kevin in South Dining Hall. He graciously answered all of my questions, even telling me that he hoped to see me at tryouts after spring break. Any doubts I had immediately flew out the window. The Leprechaun expected me to be there. I had no choice.

I couldn't help but laugh at the hodgepodge of wannabe Leprechauns I found at the tryout information session. Altogether, they represented several different stages of beard growth, a full spectrum of red hair, and various levels of commitment to an all-green wardrobe. Leprechaun Kevin greeted us, explained that tryouts would consist of two rounds of cuts, and then fielded our questions. At the end of the meeting he led us in an impromptu singing of our fight song before giving us our first task: each of us had to write a one-page essay outlining our reasons for wanting to become the next Notre Dame Leprechaun.

Daniel Colt Collins
Leprechaun Tryout Essay
2007

As far back as I can remember, people have been telling me how lucky I am. While I would like to accredit much of my success to my own skill, many point to my Irish heritage as the reason behind my good fortune. Some have even gone so far as to call me a real live leprechaun. I think of myself as somewhat similar to an energetic sprite who likes to run around, have fun, and dance jigs, so I have come to accept my status as a modern-day leprechaun.

Far before I even thought about applying to Notre Dame, I was well on my way to becoming a Fighting Irish Leprechaun. I stopped growing once I reached the ideal height of 5′6″, and I accumulated a wardrobe consisting largely of green attire. Actually, I am almost positive that I have not gone a single day without wearing something green since coming to Notre Dame. This is quite to my benefit, as most of my clothes match the emerald shine of my always-smiling Irish eyes. I have also sported a chinstrap beard ever since God blessed me with the ability to grow facial hair. In fact, I have had this same beard for so long that it now feels part of my identity. I hope that representing Notre Dame as the next Fighting Irish Leprechaun will become an even bigger part of my identity.

My first year of college has taught me that belief and inspiration stand as the most important aspects of life. If I can share that message with others and make them feel the same energy I do every time I look up at the Golden Dome, Touchdown Jesus, or Notre Dame Stadium, then I feel like I will have found my calling.

By the time I survived the first round of cuts meant to separate the Fighting Irishmen from the lads, I knew I was the best Leprechaun for the job. I just couldn't wait to get on the mic in front of a big crowd. Up to that point we had improvised only simulated game situations to a small group of cheerleaders. Our final test involved a two-minute mock pep rally speech, imitation player introductions, a live media interview, a jig-off, and a pushup contest. It would take place in front of a panel of judges from the athletic department in the basement gym of the Joyce Center known as "the pit," and it was open to the public.

The final round of tryouts coincided perfectly with Alumni Hall's signature event: Wake Week. This presented me with a slight problem, since the upperclassmen kept Wake Week shrouded in mystery and I had no idea what to expect. When final judgment day came, numerous inflatable bounce houses, a foam jousting arena, and every couch in Alumni Hall were relocated to South Quad. I had neglected my classes all week in order to concentrate on my self-assigned Leprechaun homework by learning everything there was to know about the Fighting Irish, so I didn't feel bad taking some time to enjoy the day with the rest of my Dawgs.

When it came time to focus on the task at hand, I stopped at the Grotto for a quick prayer session with my friend Meg before heading to the Joyce Center. I reflected on the opportunity that lay before me as I browsed the impressive collection of memorabilia in the concourse. The row of seven Heisman trophies neatly lined up in a glass case made me even more anxious. After a while I noticed a few other finalists milling about, so I went down into the pit to get ready.

A coat rack stood alone in a small dark room off to the side of the pit with seven dazzling green suits displayed on wire hangers. I tried on the smallest one and I could have sworn that someone had tailored it to fit me. The smallest vest even matched the blue and gold monogram tie I bought myself for this special occasion. After taking a shameless bathroom-mirror "selfie" with my phone, I read through the volumes of text messages that had been pouring in all day from friends and family. With so many people rooting for me both at Notre Dame and back home in Buffalo, I couldn't fail.

Once we all got dressed and ready to go, the cheerleaders ushered us upstairs to the hallway outside the pit. I instinctively paced back and forth while going through possible options for my speeches until I noticed everyone else doing the exact same thing. I tried to calm down by telling myself that I already had everything memorized. No use. The butterflies in my stomach kept reminding me that I would get to spend the next three years as the face of the Fighting Irish if I somehow pulled this off.

Fans with homemade signs in support of their favorite Leprechaun candidates continued to pack the pit as Leprechaun Kevin called all of us down for a group introduction. We ran out onto the freshly waxed gym floor, all of us working the crowd—jumping, clapping, jigging, and so forth. He handed us the mic one at a time, and when it came my way I nervously stuttered: "W-w-what's up I-Irish fans? I-I'm Leprechaun Dan from Buffalo, New York, and Alumni Hall!" My cheering section, the most boisterous due to the festivities of Wake Week, threw their full support behind my first feeble attempt at public Leprechauning with a "Lepre-Dan! Lepre-Dan!" chant. Leprechaun Kevin ushered us out, and I accented my exit with an extra high-flying heel click through the door.

The mock pep rally segment simulated our home opener for the following year, when our football team would square off against Georgia Tech. We went one at a time, with each of us getting two minutes to do or say whatever we wanted. I drew lucky number seven out of Kevin's magical Leprechaun hat, so I went last. Waiting for my two minutes of fame became tortuous while I watched the mixed expressions on the faces of each candidate as they emerged from the pit. I could hear muffled cheers coming from below while I paced wildly up and down the hallway like a madman. Then Leprechaun Kevin finally called my name, and a strange sense of calm washed over me as I jogged confidently down the stairs.

The crowd roared when I sprinted out into the pit while clenching my hat to prevent it from flying off my head. I reached the center of the gym floor, where I started a "Here come the Irish!" chant. It caught on nicely as I jumped back and forth, waving my arms and coaxing the crowd to get louder. Satisfied, I skipped over to the mic to say a few words.

"Notre Daaame! How's everyone feeling tonight, Irish fans?" The crowd responded perfectly with another fever pitched howl. By this point my heart had basically burst out of my chest, so I tried to regain the breath I lost during all that sprinting, jumping, and overexcitement.

"I hope you're feeling as great as I am because tomorrow is opening day in the house that Rockne built, *Notre Dame Stadium*!" I pumped my fist with each of the last three words, and the crowd went crazy yet again. I sensed they would react that way to pretty much anything I said.

"When you all come out to our stadium tomorrow and those players rush out of that tunnel, we need you to get even louder than you are here tonight. We need you to stand behind them with your full support!" I started slowly waving my arm in the signature circle motion of our opening kickoff cheer, gradually increasing its speed.

"And when we line up for that opening kickoff, I need you to get even louder! We need to show them that we're ready to start the season off strong! I need you to fill that stadium with so much energy that they can feel us shaking down the thunder all the way back in Atlanta! Come on! You came to scream tonight, so let's hear it!" I led everyone in the famous kickoff cheer, culminating in an ear-splitting "IRISH!"

"If we can do that tomorrow, those Yellow Jackets won't know what hit 'em. They'll wish they weren't goin' up against the Fightin' Irish because they'll know we came to play, we came to win, and we are...ND!" I tossed the mic to the floor, starting a "WE ARE ND!" chant while clapping in rhythm. Making one final circle around the gym, I exited with another heel click as I disappeared through the door.

Whoa...That was incredible! No time to think, though. I had only ten minutes until the next segment, and I was up first. Sweat came spilling out of every pore as raw adrenaline surged through my system. I tried to relax by taking a sip from the water fountain and chatting up my fellow finalists, but none of us could calm our nerves. We had already come too far to settle down just yet.

Before I knew it I found myself back down in the pit next to Leprechaun Kevin. He explained that I would perform a few situations for the crowd, starting with an introduction of our football captain, Travis Thomas. I walked up to the podium and gave it my best shot: "This next guy we've got coming up to speak will knock you out no matter where he is on the football field. It doesn't matter. He'll mow you down as a fierce linebacker or a bruising running back. He does it all, and you just *don't* want to get in his way. Suiting up for one more year in the blue and gold, our captain, *TRA-VIS THOMAS*!" I pumped my fist as I screamed his name and the crowd went berserk on command. That was fun. I knew I could definitely get used to that.

Kevin grabbed the mic, saying, "Now we need you to introduce Charlie Weis for us." I took the mic back without hesitation and began by pointing directly at the crowd: "This next Notre Dame Man has risen through the ranks in Fightin' Irish style. Once a fan like all of you, now the proud owner of *four* Super Bowl rings, coming back for a third year to coach his Alma Mater, we're hoping he can bring the Blue and Gold back to the glory days, our coach...*Charlieee WEIS*!" Another fist pump and another textbook reaction from the fans. I nailed it.

Next, Kevin decided to throw me a curveball by explaining that he wanted me to wish everyone in Spokane, Washington, a happy St. Patrick's Day as if I were appearing on their local news broadcast. He said I had a few minutes to think it over, but I eagerly dove right in.

"Alright, Spoka..." Silence. Shit. I had somehow pulled the mic from its cord. I attempted some diversionary arm waving, motioning for everyone to get on their feet, while someone plugged me back in. Shaking it off as best I could, I started over: "Alright, Spokane, I hope everyone has a great St. Paddy's Day this year. This time of year is dear to my heart because everyone is Irish today and I'm here with the Fightin' Irish of Notre Dame! And since it's such a special day, I have a treat for you all. I'm going to show you how to do the Notre Dame Jig. It's real easy, just follow along!" I started demonstrating the jig as performed by our students at every home game, but it didn't go over so well. Scrapping that idea, I decided to sign off: "Alright, everyone, thanks for watching and have a great St. Paddy's Day! Be safe, and don't get too crazy with that green beer!" Green beer? The judges didn't look too pleased. My friends clapped politely and I limped out of the pit to lick my wounds.

The live media interview segment came next. When my cheering section welcomed me back into the pit, their energy carried me straight past the news reporter. Leprechaun Kevin pointed me in the right direction, and I bounced over to meet Angela from one of our local stations. Without pausing for pleasantries, she started counting down to go live. The cameraman shoved his lens mere inches from my face and Angela jammed her mic into my hand.

"We're here with Leprechaun Dan, and the first question I just have to ask is whether he ate his Lucky Charms this morning."

"Of course, Angela! They're part of every Leprechaun's balanced breakfast!"

"I see. So, is that all you eat?"

"Actually, I make sure to eat from all three food groups every day: Lucky Charms, corned beef, and cabbage." That one drew a laugh from the crowd, the camera guy, and Angela. I was on a roll and I knew it.

"Alright, Leprechaun Dan, there's a lot of buzz on campus with the Blue-Gold Spring Football Game coming up. What excites you most about the Notre Dame football team this year?"

"We've got loads of fresh talent coming in: explosive freshmen for our offense and playmakers for our new defense. I'm excited, and I know all these fans behind me are ready to see what these guys can do!" The crowd backed me up with a cheer.

"Excellent, you seem to be a big football fan. With the spring season already underway, what other team should we be watching?"

My worst nightmare started to materialize as I drew a blank. After a few seconds of racking my brain, all I could think of was playing lacrosse in high school. I went with that: "Well, our lacrosse team got off to a great start. We're always a consistent contender, and we're definitely on the rise with new talent. We played well last year and we should be able to establish ourselves even more this year."

"What about baseball? They're usually dominant in their league games but they're struggling this year."

Another moment of panic…Baseball? She was joking, right? I concocted the best BS answer I could: "Well, we have a lot of young players. They make the games fun to watch, though. I really think we can turn it around for the rest of the season."

"Great. Now, I have to ask: A big drug bust on campus recently involved a Notre Dame basketball star. What are your feelings about that?"

Yep, she went there. Good thing I came prepared: "A tough situation, no doubt. The University handled it very well, though. I know the player involved remains dedicated, and his commitment to return for the Fighting Irish shows a lot about our team. I think he's going to come back and prove himself all over again."

"Let's hope so. Now, another controversial issue that may concern you personally recently resurfaced. As you may know, a lot of mascots have been under fire because they're seen as offensive or racist. The Leprechaun is a clear stereotype based on Irish people. How can you justify this?"

She asked me the one question I had been hoping for. My Irish Studies classes paid off as I went straight into scholar mode: "I'm sorry, Angela. I don't see the Leprechaun as offensive at all. In fact, our nickname represents the never-say-die attitude and the fighting mentality that Irish people have shown throughout history both in Ireland and America. Irish-Americans from South Boston to South Buffalo love our logo, and they wear it with pride even if they have no affiliation whatsoever with Notre Dame. I consider it almost like a badge of honor."

"Wow. In that case, just one more question: St. Patrick's Day just passed and you Leprechauns have a bad reputation for stealing gold. How can you condone this type of behavior while representing a Catholic university?"

The combination of wearing green and stealing gold brought back memories of my favorite story as a kid, and the perfect answer popped into my head: "Well, whenever I steal gold I always donate it back to the poor. I'm kind of like Robin Hood, only Irish." The crowd loved that one. I thanked Angela, gave one more "Go Irish!" and exited the pit with a hop, skip, and a jump.

After Angela had her way with the other finalists, we all went back down for the physical portion of our test. The song "Rakes of Mallow" crackled over the sound system, so we lined up to dance our limited edition Leprechaun Jig, a much more complicated and authentic version than the one everyone learned during freshman orientation. Once the song ended, Leprechaun Kevin asked the crowd to count off fifty pushups, one for each point we scored on senior day and another for good luck. I kept my head up with a smile on my face through all fifty, which came quite easily as a result of my still-surging adrenaline. The guy to my left began to slow down and shake a bit towards the end, but he eventually managed to grind them out along with everyone else.

With that, Leprechaun Kevin ended the show and we spent the next half hour taking photos with our friends. My cheering section, some of them proudly sporting "Team Dan" t-shirts, congratulated me on a job well done. A bunch of my Shit Alley brothers had even sacrificed several precious hours of Wake Week to stay for the entire tryout. As any Dawg would understand, that meant the world to me.

☘

I really didn't want to take that suit off, but sooner or later I had to get back into my street clothes. The judges led us up a winding staircase to a waiting area somewhere in the back recesses of the Joyce Center where we stewed as they called us into a private interview room one at a time. My turn felt more like a police interrogation, with all eight judges asking me leading questions about accountability and alcohol the entire time. They did a good job of making thirty minutes feel more like thirty years—all that because of one little "green beer" reference? When they finally released me on my own recognizance, I shuffled back to Alumni Hall, tired as a Dawg.

Leprechaun Kevin told us to look for the results posted on a single sheet of paper taped to the window outside Gate 3 of the Joyce Center around midnight. I spent the next three hours nervously sipping Guinness in Shit Alley before going to search for this mysterious sheet of paper. It gradually emerged from the darkness as I hesitantly edged my way towards Gate 3 with one hand over my eyes, but the black letters looked less and less like my name the closer I got. Two finalists *not* named Daniel Colt Collins would serve as the Gold Leprechaun at football and men's basketball games, and the Blue Leprechaun at women's basketball, soccer, and volleyball games the following year.

Disappointment consumed me for the next several hours. Two Dawg pizzas and my Flogging Molly playlist didn't make me feel any better, so I shaved my beard off in anger. No one could possibly do a better job than I could. It sucked coming so far to fall just short. I spent the rest of the night feeling sorry for myself, but when morning came I evened out my sideburns and began growing my beard back. The first cheerleading party for the new squad took place that night, and I went to congratulate both new Leprechauns. A whole year of waiting lay ahead of me, but I promised them I would win it next time.

Chapter III

Sophomore Year: The Waiting Game

SUMMER CRAWLED ALONG at a snail's pace. I just wanted to get back to my home under the Golden Dome for round two of college. A much larger room awaited my return to the Dawg House, along with three new roommates. We talked over the phone all summer long about the parties we looked forward to throwing after each Fighting Irish victory.

I got back to campus just in time for the Dawg Run. My roommate Alex brought the finest cigars from his home in Nicaragua. My other roommates Mike and Scott donned their most revealing pairs of running shorts. Our turn to do the drill sergeant thing had finally come. Carrying our oversized boom box over my head all the way across campus seemed like a good idea at first, but it turned sour real quick. So did those much-too-large cigars, which had sucked every last ounce of oxygen out of our lungs by the time we reached Stonehenge Fountain. I felt sick as a Dawg. Despite that minor hiccup and the barrage of threats thrown our way from one very angry nun as we ran through a women's dorm after visitation hours, the look on each freshman Dawg's face when we sang the Alma Mater on the steps of the Golden Dome set the tone for what would surely become a year to remember.

Football season quickly became one we wished we could forget. Our home opener against Georgia Tech, which I had been hyping up since Leprechaun tryouts began months before, didn't turn out so well. In fact, the Yellow Jackets had nothing to fear whatsoever from our blundering mess of a team. We had just witnessed the worst season-opening defeat in over 100 years of Notre Dame Football. Unwilling to take it as a sign of things to come, we threw a party anyway. After all, we had to christen 103 Alumni Hall with a celebration worthy of its new name: "The Stable."

The Hoedown Throw Down went off like a firecracker—short lived but glorious while it lasted. Country-Western décor, Astroturf carpeting, and a Toby Keith playlist provided the perfect setting for the steady flow of sophomores in cowboy and Indian attire who poured into our room. Unfortunately, our jamboree lasted all of thirty minutes before an authoritative knock on the door signaled last call. Our assassin of an assistant rector, notorious for his ability to sniff out parties from a country mile away, coldly notified us that our hootenanny had interrupted Mass in the chapel down the hall. He made sure we paid dearly in fines and service hours for our costly rookie mistake.

Undeterred, we kept partying in The Stable as a diversion from the depressing losses piling up inside Notre Dame Stadium. The way we saw it, our social gatherings provided a much-needed service for the Notre Dame community by uplifting otherwise downtrodden souls. Every loss on the football field sent a shockwave rippling through our campus. Everything from the tone of conversations in the dining halls to the general mood in classes went south. Those were dark times for us Domers. If I couldn't revive the spirit of Notre Dame as the Leprechaun, at least I could serve my community by partying for a cause.

Leprechaun Matt probably had the toughest task out of any Notre Dame Leprechaun in history. The bitterness I felt after he ousted me in tryouts faded and a sense of deep respect took hold while I watched him keep his head up through the toughest of times for Notre Dame fans everywhere. He cheered even with nothing to cheer about, doing his best to strengthen our spirit whenever it wore thin. I would always remember him as a great Notre Dame Man who worked wonders by keeping the faith alive.

My closest friends and I somehow withstood the horrors of a six-game losing streak at home, including our first loss to Navy in 43 years, by challenging ourselves to stick it out for the Alma Mater every time. Other than our only home win over lowly Duke on senior day, we pretty much had to entertain ourselves in the stands. First downs didn't come around too often, but every time they did we screamed, "Smash-mouth football!" while turning our entire section into a thrashing mosh pit. We weren't sure whether the other students around us stopped coming because they gave up on our lifeless football team, or if they relocated to avoid flying elbows to the face. Either way, we had much more breathing space by the end of the season.

I came back for the spring semester still embarrassed by the debacle of a football season I had just endured, but more eager than ever to show my Fighting Irish pride. Basketball became my outlet, and I fell in love with the Leprechaun Legion. That group of diehards would sleep overnight on cardboard laid out over a metal grate outside the Joyce Center just to make sure they watched every game from the front row of the student section. I wasn't the only one they impressed with their dedication. Head coach Mike Brey brought several piping hot pizzas to help them brave the cold before every big game. Once inside, they gave us an undeniable edge by consistently getting into our opponents' heads. I had nothing but respect for them, and I held onto the hope that one day I'd be the Leprechaun to their Legion.

In honor of Mike Brey, the one man who saved sophomore year from falling into the pits of despair, we threw a grand finale of a party prior to our Saturday afternoon showdown against our Big East rival Marquette. We ordered ten pizzas the night before, stowing them away in our fridges along with several cases of Coors. Our banquet began promptly at 8 a.m. when our friends arrived to shake off their early morning dreariness with cold pizza and beer. Just as everyone started feeling ready for some basketball, our faithful assistant rector paid us another visit. He seemed shocked to find us in the middle of a full-fledged party at 8:30 a.m., and even more shocked at the sight of our female guests. Apparently visitation hours had not yet begun for the day.

Our grand celebration came to an abrupt end, so we made our way through the snow to wait outside the Joyce Center with the Leprechaun Legion. One of our friends who had consumed many more cans of beer than slices of cold pizza repeatedly told the students in line ahead of us to go home until they got rowdier. Everyone from our party proved more than rowdy enough during the game until halftime came and our entire row fell asleep in the middle of the student section.

Ironically, my year of partying came to an end just as Wake Week began. Tryout season had returned. Time to get serious. I felt prepared for anything, a full year wiser, and ready to give it my all. Most important, I promised myself that no matter what I did I wouldn't utter the words "green beer" this time. Lucky for me, Leprechaun Matt assigned us the same essay prompt as the year before. I had already dedicated the previous several weeks to putting my thoughts into print:

Daniel Colt Collins

Leprechaun Tryout Essay

2008

When I reflect on my life I consider myself very fortunate. I have a loving family, good health, and a world of opportunity in front of me. These positive influences could be regarded as byproducts of good luck, which would coincide with the fact that I am a real live leprechaun, but I prefer to count them as blessings.

Notre Dame has blessed me with a sense of appreciation for all that life offers. This University stands as a symbol of the power that faith, devotion, and love can have when shared openly in a supportive community. As the Notre Dame Leprechaun I want to represent that uplifting spirit.

Hope is essential in life. Leprechaun Kevin and Leprechaun Matt gave all of us hope by keeping their heads up through thick and thin. They both embodied the spirit of Notre Dame. This year especially, Leprechaun Matt reminded us to enjoy the beautiful moments in life even when nothing goes as planned.

Belief drives success. Last year I wanted to be the next Notre Dame Leprechaun so I could fire up our fans and mobilize our students into a powerful force. This year I want to teach Notre Dame how to believe again.

I chose to attend Notre Dame because I recognized its unique spirit. That spirit is hard to define, but we all feel it on game days and at pep rallies. We see it on faces painted blue, gold, and green. We can find it in the eyes of every Fighting Irish fan we meet. Most important, we feel it every time members of our Notre Dame family gather together through love.

The spirit of this place has something to do with moments of pure, unadulterated happiness after impossible comeback victories, along with jigs and hugs in Stonehenge Fountain. It also has something to do with the times we must hold our heads and our golden helmets high despite tough losses. It is the reason I love Notre Dame more than I can explain. It has changed my life, and I want nothing more than to use my passion for this place to revive that spirit as the next Notre Dame Leprechaun.

I approached my second attempt at tryouts with a newfound confident swagger. When Leprechaun Matt handed me the mic for my introduction, I responded with full bravado: "How we doin' Irish fans? My name is Leprechaun Dan, named after the good ol' Irish tune 'Oh, Danny Boy,' and I currently reside in the Dawg House. I enjoy hunting Skunkbears and taking long walks through fields of four-leaf clovers."

With a whole year to plan it out, I added a few extra finishing touches to my mock pep rally as well. To demonstrate my proficiency in the art of throwing rolled-up t-shirts, an essential skill every Leprechaun must master, I brought some of my own down into the pit. When my turn came, I tossed a few to the crowd and I even placed one that I had signed as "Leprechaun Dan" on the judges' table. Bounding about on my toes, I started my go-to "Here come the Irish!" chant before dancing over to the mic to address the crowd.

"Notre Daaame! How ya feelin' tonight, Irish Fans? I'm feelin' *great* 'cause tomorrow is opening day in the house that Rockne built, *Notre Dame Stadium*!" My trusty lead-in worked so well the year before that I saw no reason to change it. The crowd agreed.

"That's right. The Skunkbears may have their Big House, those cheating Trojans may have their Coliseum, but no one...and I mean *no one*...can even come close to the tradition, the spirit, and the magic that lives in *our stadium*." The roof nearly caved in from the crowd's thunderous response.

"Some team from way out in San Diego is on its way to our campus right now, not really knowing what to expect, thinking they might just steal a win from us on the most sacred of all football fields." This time my faithful cheering section of Dawgs let out a loud "*hissss*," as I had secretly instructed them to do beforehand.

"It's up to us to make sure that never happens. The thought shouldn't even enter their minds. I know our team is ready to do just that. I'm *positive* that I'm ready to do just that. I only have one question: Are *you* ready?" Again, my Dawgs pulled through in the clutch with a chant of their own: "We're ready! We're ready! We're ready...for y'all!"

"Well then, I guess that answers it! Let's make sure they *never* forget the day they came into Notre Dame Stadium. Let's make sure they *always* remember the day they played the Fighting Irish..." This was getting way too fun. I started to lose my breath so I struck a pose. Again, they loved it. I could do no wrong.

"Let's make sure *everyone* knows who we are. That's right. We are...Notre Dame." I held the mic up high and then spiked it like I had just won a rap battle. They didn't even need my help starting a "WE ARE ND!" chant so I raced across the front row of the crowd, high fiving as I ran. I paused momentarily at the door to leave them with one final heel click out of sight. As I trotted exultantly up the stairs, I thought to myself, "*That's* how you Leprechaun!"

☘

I brought the same gusto to the rest of my tryout, never hesitating to jump right into anything Leprechaun Matt threw my way. When he asked me to introduce my favorite player on the roster during the simulation segment, I went into hype-man mode: "Alright, everybody! Check it out! I'm about to introduce you to a man who makes highlight-reel catches look *easy*. He wears number eleven because he's that much better than SportsCenter's Top 10. He's got that speed, so get ready to watch him win race after race into the end zone *all* season long. Coming at you out of Detroit, putting the *motor* in Motor City, senior wide receiver *Daviiid GRIMES*!" The crowd must not have been ready for my full-blown Michael Buffer impression. They held their cheers back a bit, almost as if they were waiting for me to belt out, "Let's get ready to rumble!"

Leprechaun Matt told me to introduce one of my favorite TV personalities, so I went with another impression: "Oh, baby! We've got a real special guest for all you basketball heads out there tonight, baby! You've probably seen him on ESPN, talkin' 'bout those diaper dandies, upset cities, and hittin' that trifecta *babyyy*! The Dukies like to think he's their biggest fan, but here at Notre Dame we know he really bleeds blue and gold. Come on, baby! Make some noise for Dicky V!" I wasn't sure if the crowd was laughing at me or with me, but I didn't care. The judges wore king-size smiles all across the board.

Everyone's favorite local news reporter, Angela, must have remembered my media interview segment from the year before. She was out to get me this time. No matter. I found my zone and let the answers flow. When she started bad-mouthing our football team for their miserable season, I came back at her with: "Hang on one second. It may have rained on us last season but, if you looked closely, you could see a rainbow through all that rain. What's at the end of that rainbow? Not my pot of gold. Nope. It's Notre Dame Stadium, and we're ready to set the gold standard this year in the house that Rock built."

Not yet satisfied after a few follow-up questions about football, she asked me to comment on a different sport. I went off: "How can I choose just one when we have so many incredible teams here? Men's and women's soccer both made deep tournament runs in the fall, men's basketball made it back to the tournament, women's basketball made it all the way to the Sweet Sixteen, hockey made it to the Frozen Four, women's tennis is on fire right now, baseball has some serious star power with the campus celebrity Sharpley brothers, and men's lacrosse is now a perennial powerhouse!"

My comebacks were too much for Angela: "Okay, okay. You clearly know your stuff. Just one more question: Where can I find your pot of gold?"

"Don't you know the Irish legend? I don't have to tell you unless you capture me! I don't think you want to try that in front of all these people though, it could get ugly." My friends broke out the catcalls and some of the judges blushed. I directed a final "Go Irish!" to the crowd as I skipped out of sight, hopeful that my self-assigned homework had just paid off.

My heart raced when the outline of that fateful white sheet of paper taped to the window outside Gate 3 took shape through the shadows. Almost afraid to look at it, I approached cautiously while peering between my fingers. I said a Hail Mary as the hazy outline of two names became clearer. There it was. My name printed in bold black ink next to the words "Blue Leprechaun." I wasn't sure whether I let out a shout for joy or a sigh of relief. Whatever it was, it felt incredible.

My eyes scanned the words over and over to make sure they weren't a mirage, and I even snapped a photo just in case my name somehow disappeared. After several return trips to the window for verification, I called to tell my mom that I was the next Notre Dame Leprechaun for women's basketball, soccer, and volleyball. Her inaudibly high-pitched response brought me out of my state of shock and I began jumping around by myself in the darkness. My dad responded in similar fashion, minus the shrill screaming.

I spent my first few moments as a Notre Dame Leprechaun with my brothers in The Stable. We threw a spontaneous victory celebration, complete with more top-shelf Nicaraguan cigars. I answered a call from an unknown number, and Leprechaun Juan greeted me with, "Congrats, partner!" I told him how humbled I was by the opportunity to learn from the first international student in history to serve as the Gold Leprechaun. More friends stopped by my room to wish me well. We blasted Irish music and danced the night away.

As soon as I stepped through the front door into the post-tryout cheerleading party, several hands immediately hoisted me into the air. I knew I was in trouble when they carried me upside down towards a bright orange five-gallon jug on the kitchen counter. Raising my legs into the air, they positioned my head in front of the spout and let the contents of that cooler loose like the opening of a floodgate. I chugged as fast as I could just to keep up with the flow of whatever purple concoction began streaming down each corner of my mouth while everyone counted out the seconds. A few too many passed by before I finally tapped out.

Before I even had a chance to catch my breath, I found myself hoisted into the air once again. This time they threw me on top of the pool table in the middle of the main room. Several past Leprechauns joined me and, without warning, someone kicked in the front door. The unmistakably shrill blaring of bagpipes met our ears as a man with an enormous handlebar mustache and a kilt stepped through the doorframe while playing our fight song. Barely believing my eyes, I reacted to the ridiculousness of what just happened in the same way that any Leprechaun would. I danced around the pool table while everyone belted out the lyrics. The piper continued with "Rakes of Mallow," and a miracle must have prevented that pool table from falling through the floor due to the force of twenty feet ferociously jigging in unison. We had an Irish celebration for the ages. Endless hugs and Irish toasts filled the rest of my blurry first night as a Notre Dame Leprechaun. I knew I was in for one wild ride.

Chapter IV

Junior Year: Learning to Leprechaun

STUDYING ABROAD between sophomore and junior years gave me the perfect opportunity to practice my Leprechaun pose in front of every famous landmark in Ireland. On top of that, I got to experience the breathtaking beauty of the Emerald Isle. The grass grew green, the Guinness flowed pure, and rich storytelling oozed from every pub. I was living the dream of not only every Leprechaun, but every one of my fellow Irish history nerds back at Notre Dame.

When I returned to campus in the fall, I soon found out that life as the Blue Leprechaun wasn't all glitz and glamour. Almost immediately, I grew tired of the disappointed looks on the faces of everyone I met after having to explain that I technically wasn't the actual Leprechaun, but more of a back-up bootleg version. Even the daily grind seemed daunting. I couldn't believe that my new duties as one of the foremost representatives of my

University included bagging the cheerleaders' dirty laundry, going to mandatory cheerleading practices every day, and waking up before dawn twice a week to embarrass myself amongst the hulking behemoths in the varsity weight room.

As much as I liked to complain, life could've been much worse. My fellow cheerleaders never ceased to surprise me with their constant optimism. The girls reminded me of little Energizer Bunnies hopping around with endless pep. Even if I didn't do too much other than stand around for most of our two-hour practices, I couldn't help but feel uplifted by such motivated and generally happy people. The dynamics of a team filled with six tiny girls, six huge guys, and two goofy Leprechauns got weird sometimes, but our mutual love for Notre Dame brought us together like one big happy family.

It became easier to appreciate all the behind-the-scenes work that went into being a mascot once the school year got underway. My first official appearances involved teaching the incoming freshmen all of our cheers in preparation for their first football season inside Notre Dame Stadium. I even had the honor of giving our eager new students their first homework assignments: to learn the words of our fight song and Alma Mater by game time on Saturday. From that point on I heard passing whispers of "Oh, my god! It's the Leprechaun!" pretty much every time I walked across campus.

While I didn't necessarily try to keep a low profile, I never went out of my way to unveil my alter ego either. I had more fun letting the topic come up on its own through casual conversation. Coordinating my schedule proved difficult early on, so I often brought my leprechaun suit to class carefully folded away in a gym bag. Our world-renowned political science professor, Sebastian Rosato, must have noticed the bright green hat sitting on top of my bag one day because he stopped mid-lecture to ask, "Daniel, would you please share your secret identity with the class?" After turning a few different shades of red, I stammered through the quick explanation I had prepared should such a moment arise. He paused for a moment before following up with, "Do you mean to tell me that you rule the world of mascots like I rule the world of political scientists?" Priceless moments like that made the painstakingly repetitive comments I heard on a regular basis about good luck, pots of gold, rainbows, and Lucky Charms more than worth it.

As always, life changed drastically once football season began. The hoopla surrounding our home games sometimes got too hectic to handle, but I loved every second of every weekend. The swelling crowds would spill into every quad at a steady pace as I stared out the window during my Friday afternoon class. Every clock on campus seemed to tick away in slow motion until 4 p.m. when I got to make an official appearance at a "bookstore rally" in order to motivate our loyal shoppers to spend, spend, spend in support of the Fighting Irish. A posse of cheerleaders would follow me into the bookstore as I led them in a "Here come the Irish!" chant, and then I would give a thirty-second speech about how badly our football team was about to beat whatever opponent we happened to play the next day. We always finished with a "WE ARE ND!" chant before our two minutes of glory gave way to at least two hours of posing for photos with fans. Since the Gold Leprechaun spent all afternoon preparing for the Friday night pep rally, I was the first Leprechaun most of our fans had a chance to meet. They gathered around me in droves, and I watched in amazement every time they instinctively formed a single-file line stretching all the way out the door.

I always laughed at the panicked state most fans found themselves in when their moment to snap a picture with me finally came after twenty minutes of standing in line. Completely frazzled, they would instantly forget how to use whatever device they had planned to capture the moment with. This inevitably frustrated their kids, who would yell at them out of embarrassment until they finally figured out how to take a photo. I had never seen anyone more consistently upset and downright mean than teenagers reacting to their parents who just couldn't find it within themselves to successfully navigate the intricacies of a digital camera. I tried to do everything in my power to make sure such recurring family feuds didn't end up ruining otherwise perfect pilgrimages to Notre Dame.

Patience became a valuable virtue, and I made sure to tell every flustered fan not to worry because I wasn't going anywhere. Greeting them all individually, I would introduce myself, ask their names, and share several hearty handshakes. That usually got them smiling. The Leprechaun pose also worked wonders at diffusing even the most hostile situations. Everyone seemed to get a kick out of posing next to me with their fists raised, and I loved seeing the crazy variations they came up with. Some would stand straight up and hold their arms out wide over their heads, some would crouch down real low and touch their fists together in front of their faces, and every once in a while someone would pull off the perfect Fighting Irish stance.

One groundbreaking phenomenon that I discovered while posing for pictures involved the inexplicable trend of women wanting to hand me their babies. For some reason they all assumed that I knew how to properly hold an infant. I never understood that. Leprechauns were supposedly notorious for causing mischief, yet mothers constantly entrusted their newborns to me without even the slightest hesitation. Whenever a family decided to take a group shot with me, I almost always ended up holding the baby. After each bookstore rally, I tried to guess how many more Christmas cards on refrigerators and framed family portraits hanging over mantels would soon feature me proudly displaying a small child in my arms.

As much as taking photos with fans seemed glamorous, it sometimes felt like prom dragged out over the course of an entire weekend. Every time I appeared anywhere on campus, an impromptu line formed for more pictures. It became impossible to get from point A to point B, so we instituted the "Leprechaun duty rule" that required one male cheerleader to stay with me at all times. Whenever the crowd got out of hand he would take one for the team by turning into the bad guy and pulling me away. With his help I could escape without ever having to reject any fans. The system worked perfectly as long as whoever had Leprechaun duty remembered to do his job. Otherwise I would find myself stranded with a constantly multiplying horde closing in around me, hopelessly unable to break free.

Despite the difficulty of dealing with big crowds, I relished the opportunity to help fans create lasting memories. I posed for thousands upon thousands of photos, but I knew every fan had their own story and each picture may have meant the world to at least one of them. Contributing in my own small way to the positive influence that Notre Dame had on their lives left me feeling deeply honored. I got so caught up in my weekly quest to take as many pictures and sign as many autographs as I could that I usually lost all track of time. When my first football weekend as the Blue Leprechaun came to a close I noticed that my face, thighs, and forearms ached terribly. It seemed like a strange combination, and I had no idea what caused the pain. Not until the following week did I realize that my cheeks hurt from smiling so much and the rest of my pain came from squatting down in the Leprechaun pose for hours on end. I told myself that soreness from an overzealous smiling and posing workout probably wasn't something to complain about.

As much as I wanted to get involved, football was Leprechaun Juan's gig. If I didn't have my own teams to worry about, I probably would have turned green with Leprechaun envy when he flew out to Los Angeles to shoot a commercial, or when he spent Christmas vacationing at the Hawaii Bowl. Luckily, our women's soccer team saved me from such jealousy. After every bookstore rally, I watched Juan emcee the Friday night pep rally from a distance before making my way to Alumni Stadium for some soccer.

My love affair with women's soccer escalated quickly. Our team had class, character, toughness, and heart. I had just finished studying abroad over the summer with my classmates Amanda Clark and Haley Ford, so watching them play lockdown defense all season was a blast. Another classmate, Michele Weissenhofer, became a spectacle with her signature flip throws, as did rising freshman sensation, Melissa Henderson, who had a knack for getting to the net. Our goalie, Kelsey Lysander, consistently put on a show as she rarely ever gave up a goal, finishing her career without losing a single game she started at Notre Dame. I even began to understand why the rest of the world called soccer "the beautiful game" when I witnessed senior co-captains Brittany Bock and Kerri Hanks completely control the action every time they took the field. They had to be the easiest team in the world to cheer for, and their fans made my job as their mascot even more fun. These weren't average college sports fans, either. The diehard locals never needed any help starting cheers, and Goshen College students sang Euro-style soccer songs throughout the entirety of every home game. Altogether, the whole scene created a sense of purity rarely found in big-time athletics anymore.

I watched more than my fair share of brilliant moments from my designated spot on the sidelines while the girls extended their undefeated season deep into the playoffs. Kerri Hanks picked the perfect moment to come back from her sprained MCL when she entered our second-round playoff game, ripped her knee brace off as the ball came her way, threw it to the sideline, then assisted the game-winning goal. No one in Alumni Stadium could believe what they had just seen. When it came time to host Minnesota in the quarterfinals, head coach Randy Waldrum offered free hot chocolate to every fan who braved the subzero wind chill. Even after spending my childhood shoveling cars out of snowbanks in Buffalo, I never knew what bitter cold felt like until that night. I didn't even feel guilty sneaking some Baileys Irish Cream into my hot chocolate just to survive. My shillelagh snapped like a frozen twig against the icy bleachers when I let it fly in celebration of our sudden game-winning goal just as overtime started. I didn't mind taping it back together because that goal meant only two more wins separated us from a national championship.

Every high-school girls' soccer team in the state of North Carolina must have made the trip to Raleigh for the Final Four. The constant swarm surrounding me throughout the entire semifinal game earned me the nickname "teen heartthrob" for the rest of our trip. I took credit for our win when I refused to take pictures with any of them unless they promised to cheer us on. It didn't take long until "Let's go Irish!" echoed throughout the stadium. After the win, we met our team outside the tunnel to congratulate them before heading back to the hotel for a victory party of our own.

Since the soccer girls wisely chose to stay focused on the national championship game scheduled for the following evening, the cheerleaders and I decided to celebrate extra hard in their honor. Two cases of Coors and several hotel mini garbage cans full of ice found their way into the bathtub in my room prior to our team dinner at a Hibachi restaurant. Then one innocent sake-bomb led to several exotic cocktails ending up at our table. Sixty Silver Bullets with frosty blue mountains welcomed us back when we squeaked in just before curfew. The string of toasts we raised to our soccer team and their upcoming national championship lasted until dawn.

The rude ringing of an unanticipated wake-up call interrupted my sweet slumber at precisely 8:30 a.m., after which I rolled over to find a four-tiered "beer-amid" stacked with precision on my nightstand. We had fifteen minutes until our bus left for Sunday morning Mass. Perfect. The twelve-dollar bottle of Evian I gulped down did little to loosen the vice grip crushing my skull, so I took a cold shower and threw on my Sunday best. Before leaving, we decided to get rid of any evidence left over from our revelry the night before. My teammate Charles drew the short straw, so we sent him out into the hallway to dispose of a bulging garbage bag filled with empty cans. Less than thirty seconds passed by before he came clamoring back into the room still holding the bag and looking like he had just seen a ghost. Apparently, once he reached the end of the hallway he found himself face to face with our athletic director. Rather than play it cool, he froze like a deer in headlights before hightailing it back to our room. After explaining why that probably wasn't the smartest course of action, we convinced him to carry the bag out to a dumpster while we boarded the bus.

We made it to the nearest Catholic church only fifteen minutes into Mass, but the ushers still felt the need to make us atone for our sins by relegating us to the upper balcony. It had to be over a hundred degrees up there. The sweltering heat didn't mix with my splitting headache too well, and my whole world got foggy when I turned to share the sign of peace with my teammates. I tried to ask Charles for help, but only an unintelligible jumble came out. Everything moved like molasses and I felt like I was walking on the moon as I impolitely pushed past my teammate Adam. The whole cheerleading squad watched in horror as I staggered past aisles of pews on my way towards the door. The last thing I remembered was Adam asking how I felt, then everything went black. I woke up to our captain Dave propping me up in the doorway. Fully revived from my quick nap and a breath of fresh air, I rejoined our squad in time for the Eucharist.

Plenty of rest and loads of southern soul food recharged

my batteries in time for the national championship game that night. Unsurprisingly outnumbered by UNC fans, we tried our best to be heard. Our team fought hard, even taking an early lead, but a late surge by the Tar Heels sent a sizzling hot spear through my heart when it ruined our dream season. I really felt for our girls. They gave me my first glimpse at just how powerfully Notre Dame could influence so many lives even as far away from campus as North Carolina. Our student newspaper, *The Observer,* published part of the letter I wrote them after their final game:

> To the 2008 Notre Dame Women's Soccer Team:
>
> "Football" is known as the beautiful game. I never understood what that meant until I saw the way you played this year. When I look back, I remember good times and amazing moments. I remember the thousands of young soccer players who watched you in awe, dreaming of suiting up for the Fighting Irish one day. I remember the diehard fans who faithfully made it to every game, cheering you by name until their voices went hoarse. I remember a packed house during the coldest night on record, with our student section going crazy for all ninety-plus minutes of an overtime thriller. Most of all, I remember how you brought the same fire to every game. You played with genuine pride, and the inspiration you generated will continue on long after you leave Notre Dame. I have never seen a team like this before in any sport. During a time when we all tend to lose sight of what representing something greater than ourselves is all about, you showed us

that sports can still be pure. To the coaching staff, the trainers, and the entire team: Thanks for keeping the spirit alive. Go Irish!

Once soccer season ended, I went back to my Buffalo roots by becoming the first Leprechaun ever to appear on the ice at a Notre Dame hockey game. I had watched every home game since my freshman year from those collapsible temporary bleachers inside the Joyce Center fieldhouse. No other team amassed more wins during that stretch than Notre Dame under the tutelage of our consummate head coach, Jeff Jackson. Not wanting to surrender my perfect attendance record, I asked his promotions team if I could get involved as their Leprechaun. It was a match made in hockey heaven.

Prior to the construction of the monumental Compton Ice Arena with its colossal video screens and special effects, we implemented a simple strategy to generate excitement during our home games. I greeted each fan with a "Go Irish!" as I handed out cowbells to shake noisily after every goal, and then I chose four lucky contestants to join me at center ice for a shoot-out contest between periods. My signature trick consisted of sliding across the ice after a running start with one of our giant blue and gold flags trailing in my wake. I loved playing such an integral role in a program clearly on the rise. We started from scratch, but ended up watching the energy we created escalate into a riotous scene by the end of the season. With help from the hockey pep-band, who always let the opposing goalie know that every goal we scored was "all his fault," we turned that makeshift arena into a madhouse. I was proud of my legacy, and I hoped future Leprechauns would continue the tradition.

While I enjoyed my leading role in the smalltime production of Notre Dame Hockey, I stepped wide-eyed into the professionally run three-ring circus known as Notre Dame Women's Basketball. Legendary coach Muffet McGraw set the tone for every home game with a different pair of stunning stilettos. Not only had she already established a powerhouse of a program, but her promotions staff turned her franchise into Michiana's top-ranked family activity. They constantly had me on the go, refereeing children's rubber-chicken-throwing matches, delivering endless prizes to lucky fans, judging which section cheered loudest during timeouts, and getting thrown into human pyramids with the cheerleaders. We even held up giant signs that said "Big Mac" to get the crowd keyed up for free burgers every time the girls scored more than 88 points in a single game. My favorite promotions stunt of all time came when I got to assist the timeless wonder known as the Red Panda while she flipped ceramic bowls onto her head during her death-defying unicycle act.

A different breed of fans filled the seats for women's basketball. They came to enjoy the family atmosphere and simply have a good time. Very few of them ever left a game feeling disappointed, but that probably had more to do with our unstoppable team than any of my efforts. Either way, each game gave me a safe place to practice interacting with fans without fearing rejection. They provided the perfect environment for a Gold Leprechaun in training, and they taught me the most critical lesson I could have learned: people will do pretty much anything for a free t-shirt.

Stubborn fans would sit like bumps on a log without showing the slightest inclination of joining in the fun going on around them but, as soon as I ran onto the court carrying a rolled-up t-shirt, their inner five-year-olds would come out as they jumped up and down while screaming, "Me, me, me!" I wasn't exactly handing out luxury apparel, either. These were extra-large, extra-tacky white shirts with huge sponsor logos printed all over them. None of that mattered. If I wanted to get fans on their feet and I had to choose between Melissa Lechlitner hitting a clutch game-winning three-pointer at the buzzer or a free t-shirt flying through the air, I would bet on the shirt every single time.

Women's basketball left me with one of my fondest memories as the Blue Leprechaun. Our trip to Hartford, Connecticut, for the Women's Big East Tournament got off to a rocky start with a 4:30 a.m. bus ride from South Bend to Chicago, followed by a drawn-out full day of delayed flights and every other travel-related frustration possible.

I stomped into our hotel in Hartford at 9:30 p.m. tired, hungry, and looking more like Oscar the Grouch than a Leprechaun. Six huge male cheerleaders and I went on a hunger-induced rage when our waiter refused to serve us at a brewpub because it was after 9 p.m., I was underage, and none of them were my parents. He cowered in fear as my teammate and future fireman Don huffed and puffed his way out the front door.

Every restaurant host and hostess in Hartford responded with the same "no room at the inn" excuse when they found out I was twenty years old until finally a bouncer let me slide for ten bucks. I swore I only wanted something to eat, but our waitress felt bad when everyone else ordered adult beverages so she poured me one on the house. Not wanting to hurt her feelings, I enjoyed my frothy brew with the rest of the fellas. Just as I tipped my pint back to finish it off, I caught a glimpse of the red-faced bouncer storming towards me with smoke billowing from his ears. I didn't put up much of a fight when he asked if I had been drinking, but when he motioned for me to follow him towards the kitchen, I realized I needed an exit strategy. I found the break I was looking for when he turned his back for no more than a split second. My teammates said they could hear me screaming from a mile away as I ran out the front door all the way back to the hotel.

After deciding to retire early for the night, I woke up the next morning with brighter eyes and a bushier tail than the rest of the cheerleaders as we sent our basketball team off to the XL Center with an *a cappella* rendition of the fight song. The arena lived up to its name, and the butterflies in my stomach came alive when I peeked out at the size of the crowd from the loading bay where we waited with all of the other cheerleaders. I didn't see anyone rushing over to take pictures with any other mascots, but quite a few cheerleaders told me they just *had* to get a photo with me so they could show it to their relatives who loved Notre Dame more than anything. I made sure they all betrayed their school colors by doing the Leprechaun pose with me. Even Rocky, the USF Bull, joined in by jumping into my arms for an exclusive photo opp.

My nervousness deflated into disappointment when the arena ushers restricted me to a two-foot square taped out on the floor by the end line during our entire matchup against DePaul. They blamed their unwillingness to negotiate on tournament rules. Even though we warmed up all those stunts backstage, they only let us go out onto the court during one timeout each half. I made the best of a bad situation by heckling the Lady Blue Demons all game long from within the confines of my tiny imaginary cage. After the easy victory, I jogged over to high-five some Fighting Irish fans in the front row. A woman stopped me to say that her daughter had just applied to Notre Dame, so I flipped her one of the lucky gold coins I kept in my pocket at all times. Her face lit up and she told me the gift would make her daughter's day. Once again, the awesomeness of making a big difference by doing something so small stepped right up and smacked me in the face.

Still out of breath but beaming as I sauntered through

the tunnel, I found myself cornered by an ESPN intern with a hand-held video camera. She fired off a series of questions about Notre Dame Women's Basketball, the Big East Tournament, Hartford, and my new favorite holiday, Saint Patrick's Day. I did the best I could while gasping for air and looking around for some water. She probably should have warned me that a video featuring a disheveled-looking Leprechaun clearly panting while performing a sloppy jig would find its way onto ESPN.com for the next three weeks.

Unhappy with the local restaurant scene, we took a trip to Boston for dinner at a legendary McIrish pub called The Black Rose. As much as I wanted to try one of their perfectly poured pints of Guinness, I steered clear after my near escape the night before. Instead, I ate green ice cream out of a Red Sox mini-helmet while we toured Fenway Park before heading back to our hotel in Hartford. When we got off the bus, a group of kids wearing homemade Golden Dome hardhats welcomed us with eager applause. One little guy insisted that I take his green Sharpie as a token of gratitude after I signed his basketball jersey. From then on, I never left home without one.

The next morning we continued our new tradition of sending the team off to the arena by singing the fight song. This time our band joined in by playing "Rakes of Mallow" and the basketball girls stopped to dance a quick jig with us. West Virginia's Mountaineer mascot and his crew of cheerleaders happened to watch the whole spontaneous dance party from the hotel lobby. He turned Irish green with envy at the sight of us having way too much fun. Either that, or his itchy beard and constricting buckskin pants put him in a bad mood.

Villanova's mascot "Will D. Cat" made up for the Mountaineer's lack of spirit when I challenged him to a game of one-on-one in the arena before our teams came out for warm-ups. To be fair, his suit probably weighed close to forty pounds with a huge foam head adding on another ten. Still, I looked like a Harlem Globetrotter out there with my crossovers and behind-the-back spin moves. Our fans went wild until I air-balled a fadeaway and the big cat swatted my second attempt at a mid-range jumper. I decided to retire and stick to Leprechauning.

We ended up taking an early exit in the second round after falling victim to the three-ball, but I could have sworn the hoop on Villanova's side of the court looked bigger than ours. Our cheerleading squad probably took the loss harder than the actual basketball team. When our chaperone wanted to take us out to a certain brewpub to help us shake it off, we convinced her to look elsewhere after realizing she planned to bring us back to the scene of my run-in with the now-infamous red-faced bouncer. We settled on Morton's and, $1,200 later, the whole squad thanked me for their steak.

The cheerleaders and I turned every trip into an adventure, every game into a party, and every magic Notre Dame moment into a shared memory. Nothing could top our volunteer work, though. With no cumbersome foam head to worry about, my leprechaun suit allowed me to connect with fans on a personal level. With a mission rooted in service, Notre Dame allowed me to become more than just a mascot. Sometimes the giant arenas, massive crowds, thousands of photos, and endless autographs could inflate our egos just a bit, but none of us ever experienced anything as humbling as serving others while representing our University.

When Saint Patrick's Day came, I had the good fortune of meeting the fantastic staff at Bittersweet Branch Library in Mishawaka, Indiana. They set me up with a bag full of chocolate gold coins and the perfect book for the occasion—*Jamie O'Rourke and the Big Potato: An Irish Folktale* by Tomie dePaola. Thirty of their children's reading program all-stars sat cross-legged with anxious smiles while I read aloud in full Leprechaun garb. After we all found out what ended up happening to poor ol' Jamie, I got them on their feet for an Irish jig lesson. I demonstrated the steps a few times by counting them off real slow, and they seemed to pick up on it right away.

I could only watch helplessly when the music came on and the madness unfolded around me. Two or three girls must have been Irish dancers because they put my footwork to shame. Other than that, most of the "jigging" consisted of hopping wildly up and down, jumping off of chairs, and running in circles. A sudden flick of the lights had them all back in position sitting cross-legged once again, and I shared my super-secret lucky-leprechaun stash of Saint Patrick's gold.

Our question and answer session started off relatively

straightforward, with the conversation focusing mostly on good luck and the color green. Then one boy raised his hand to tell me how much his brother liked Notre Dame. A girl followed his lead by raising her hand to tell me how much her dad liked Notre Dame. One by one, they all proceeded to tell me how much they liked chocolate, dancing, reading, coloring, candy, horses, tractors, and big trucks. One boy even told me how much he liked the University of Michigan. I hated to see such a bright young man with his whole life ahead of him headed down the wrong path at such an early age.

The weather finally broke and my year as the Blue Leprechaun began to wind down, but not before my teammate Jenny approached me with a special request. She proudly served as one of the two girls on our cheerleading squad selected each year from our esteemed sister school Saint Mary's College. SMC hosted an annual dance marathon to benefit Riley Children's Hospital of Indiana. They raised money by pledging to remain on their feet for twelve straight hours in honor of children who were unable to do so. Jenny planned on adding an extra spark by showing up in her cheerleading uniform, so she asked me to come along in my green suit.

We arrived at the large gym already packed with hundreds of SMC students impressively dedicating their Friday nights to making a difference. I felt refreshed by what I saw, and I thanked the event president, Sarah, for including me. Then I met my new hero, Austin—a fearless fourteen-year-old destroyer of cancer. When he approached me in his wheelchair I knew he had Notre Dame Football on his mind. We talked for almost an hour about our favorite team's prospects for the next season. He told me not to worry because he knew we would turn it around sooner or later. My tears became increasingly hard to hide while I listened to his effortless optimism. I thought about the hope and excitement that Notre Dame Football brought into his life on a daily basis, and I wondered if our football players knew they were playing for Austin and millions more like him every time they strapped on their golden helmets.

Austin calmly cut our conversation short when the SMC staff invited him up on stage to give a talk. He needed no prep time whatsoever to deliver a speech that floored everyone in the gym, telling us that he cheered for the Fighting Irish because of their long history of always fighting without ever giving up. He said he tried to remember that mentality every day so he could do the same in his own life. I couldn't imagine anyone more deserving of a standing ovation, and not a dry eye remained in the house when he stood up from his wheelchair to tip his Notre Dame ball cap to the gathering crowd. He left all of us speechless, and I felt honored to kneel next to him while we both struck the Leprechaun pose for a photo opp.

My life was a perfect mix of celebration and service. Notre Dame sent me out into the world to smile, have fun, share joy, and spread goodwill. It wasn't a bad gig. I met countless kindhearted volunteers and I learned from some pretty amazing people with even more amazing stories. It all made me realize why I put up with hauling dirty laundry, lifting weights at 6 a.m., and standing around at cheerleading practice for two hours every day while my schoolwork piled up. I did it for the chance to meet a hero like Austin, exchange a spirited "Go Irish!" or even just a simple smile, and feel the spirit of Notre Dame at work as it changed another life.

Tryout season snuck up on us once again, and Leprechaun Juan reluctantly prepared to pass the lucky shillelagh down to another deserving Fighting Irishman. During his reign as the Gold Leprechaun, he had mastered the art of putting full effort into every moment, no matter how small. In the process he taught me how to find joy in even the least likely aspects of life. They were only size seven, but he left some pretty big shoes to fill. I felt ready:

> Daniel Colt Collins
> Leprechaun Tryout Essay
> 2009
>
> I will always remember the first time I experienced the spirit of Notre Dame. After visiting campus I fell in love with the pride, happiness, and uniquely positive outlook that everyone seems to share here. Still, I had no idea what to expect when I arrived at the opening pep rally during freshman

orientation. I found myself instantly overcome with emotion when the band came marching in to the tune of our fight song with a force unlike anything I had ever heard before. The entire crowd stood up and began clapping while a unifying energy swept over all of us. I couldn't quite understand why, but I felt like I was on the verge of laughter and tears at the same time. Right then and there, I knew I had come to the right place.

The same feelings came over me again a few weeks later when I experienced the magic that surrounds every Notre Dame football game. I took it all in: the pep rally, the drum circle, the players walking from the Basilica to Notre Dame Stadium, and the crowds lining sidewalks to cheer on our band. Campus came alive. Inside Notre Dame Stadium our collective anticipation built higher and higher until it finally burst with an explosion of raw emotion when the football team rushed out onto the field. As I saw our Leprechaun and cheerleaders proudly leading the way—with a shining wave of golden helmets spilling out into the sun behind them—I realized that my love for Notre Dame represented a much deeper power. I wanted nothing more than to immerse myself in that power and fuel it with my energy as the next Notre Dame Leprechaun.

My heart dropped right out of my chest when my name failed to appear on that list. I didn't count it as a defeat, though. Instead, I promised myself that I would embrace the Fighting Irish mentality until I finally proved myself. Another year of watching and waiting taught me the value of patience coupled with optimism. I came back driven by the same power. Still, I felt nothing but pure terror as I approached that list for the second time. Then my dread gave way to a wild rush of excitement and relief when I discovered my name alongside the words "Blue Leprechaun."

From the first moment I tried on my very own custom green three-piece suit until now, I have made enough unforgettable memories to last a lifetime. "Leprechauning" is all about living in the moment with a heart full of joy, sincerity, and a whole lot of energy. It's all about changing lives through the simplest of acts, like reading stories to groups of young kids or talking about Notre Dame Football with courageous cancer patients.

My experiences as a Domer over the past three years and as a Leprechaun this past year have prepared me for my final chapter at Notre Dame. If given the chance, I feel ready to bring new energy to the Gold Leprechaun position, add more "fight" and more "Irish" to the Fighting Irish, and leave my own legacy as a contribution to the spirit that I fell in love with when I first came to this hallowed place.

Wake Week returned to the Dawg House, once again coinciding with the final round of Leprechaun tryouts. After a few days of partaking in the festivities, I escaped to the Morris Inn for some peace and quiet on the eve of my final attempt at becoming the Gold Leprechaun. I checked my mailbox before leaving Alumni Hall with my toothbrush and pillow. An envelope from my dad contained a handwritten note:

> Good luck with tryouts, Dan. What does it feel like to become the Notre Dame Leprechaun? I imagine that it feels like a combination of more glory, adventure, magic, gratitude, gladness, and humility than any other man can experience in a lifetime. How do I know? That's what it feels like to be your dad. Peace and Love.

My game face came out early on Friday, April 25, 2009, when I suited up in green to give it one last shot. With my dad's words echoing in my head, I sat stoically in the hallway above the pit while six other apprehensive wannabe Leprechauns scurried about. I came dangerously close to taking myself way too seriously, but that very same political science professor who had called me out months before stepped in unexpectedly to save the day. He happened to walk by just moments before we went out in front of the crowd and, when he saw me, he said I'd better liven up because I looked like death. I jokingly thanked him for the sarcastic advice, but his words actually snapped me out of my much-too-businesslike attitude. I hadn't gotten that far by treating it like a chore. From day one I promised myself to have fun with it. Everything I had planned flew out the window. This was no time to put on an act. I ran down into the pit confident, happy, and free. Jimmy Ryan would have been proud.

My fellow Dawg and cheerleading teammate Mike set the tone for tryouts by introducing us while still on cloud nine from Wake Week. He turned it into a lighthearted affair when he began mocking us right away. When he called my name, I responded with, "What's up everyone? I'm Leprechaun Dan. I hail from West Cork, Ireland, and I currently live in Alumni Hall. I enjoy making wooden shoes, hording gold, and walking through fields of four-leaf clovers." Mike made fun of every single thing I said except the Alumni Hall part. Then he started a "Where my Dawgs at?" chant to the delight of our friends in the crowd.

I went second in the mock-pep-rally round, right after my other fellow Dawg and cheerleading teammate Charles. He definitely had the heart of a Leprechaun, but he admitted several times beforehand that he felt too tall and too Italian to serve as a full-time authentic Fighting Irishman. His turn must have gone well because he ran back up from the pit laughing and making sure to tell everyone in sight just how much fun he was having. Happy that he warmed up the crowd for me, I leapt down the stairs to have my turn.

Rather than sprint around until I could barely breathe, I walked with a slow swagger across the gym floor to the front of the crowd. Just as I expected, everyone waited silently for my next move. One of my friends, still proudly sporting his Wake Week boxers and necktie, yelled out, "Do something already!" The gym echoed with laughter. I reached into my pockets, pulled out thirteen lucky gold coins, and flung them over my head into the crowd. A mad scramble ensued until they realized the coins were plastic. Mic in hand, I took a step back to get started.

"Notre Daaame! Make some *noise*!" Notre Dame did.

"Now let me hear you crank it up just one time! Get your arms up! On three: One, two, three! Crank! Me! Up!" The crowd knew what to do. Sergio Brown had become a fan favorite during the previous football season with his back-flip celebrations and his signature "Crank me up!" chant.

"One more time...like you mean it! Arms up! Come on judges, you too! One, two, three! Crank! Me! Up!" They sounded much more unified that time. Even the judges followed my lead. Satisfied, I got on with my speech.

"I like the sound of that, and you can plan on gettin' it crankin' in the house that Rockne built *all* season long this year. You know why? I'll tell you why. There's a reason this is the best place *on earth* to play football. There's a reason the name *Notre Dame* carries that power with it *wherever* it's heard. There's a reason our *tradition* is so strong. That reason is *you*!" I pointed at my Dawgs with that last word and they went bananas.

"You've all seen The Shirt this year, right? You know how it says, 'Defend Our Honor' across the back? Well consider that a call to arms—not just for our football team, but to each and every one of *you*!" Another finger pointed towards my Dawgs got them going gorillas.

"Now I wanna hear what you're gonna sound like in a couple months when Notre Dame is *beating Southern Cal* in *our* stadium and *our* defense is on the field defending *our* honor!" Absolute anarchy ensued, followed by a frothy-mouthed "Beat SC!" chant. Without really meaning to, I had just started a full-blown war rally. Rather than get out of there while I still could, I decided to crowd surf. My Dawgs almost tore me to shreds. The judges looked worried when I finally freed myself from their clutches with my tie undone and my shirt nearly ripped off. Exhausted and sweating profusely, I managed one last signature heel-click through the door on my way out.

Juan set the scene for me when I came back down into the pit for my situation segment. He told me to imagine myself on the court in Madison Square Garden while the Fighting Irish trailed Pittsburgh late in a Big East Tournament game. We needed a defensive stop, and I had to make sure the crowd did their part. Without hesitation I started a "Gooo Irish! Beeeat Panthers!" chant, followed by my go-to "Here come the Irish!"

Putting me to the test, Juan then told me to introduce Johnny Lattner to the crowd. I had met Johnny at a tailgate a few months earlier, so I went with an embellished version of our encounter: "Our next guest confused me at a tailgate in the stadium parking lot last fall when he asked if I wanted to meet his good friend 'Little Johnny.' Without waiting for an answer, he held up the Heisman he won back in 1953. Yes, he named the trophy after himself. He can get away with that, though, because he used to make highlight reel plays before highlight reels even existed. Ladies and gentlemen, please welcome legendary Notre Dame halfback, Johnny Lattner!" My somewhat true story paid off. I made a mental note to thank Little Johnny and real Johnny for their help.

Each Leprechaun candidate had to act out one final introduction to wrap up the situation segment. Jimmy Clausen had just broken every record in the book during the Hawaii Bowl, so introducing him came easy: "Rumor has it our athletic director Jack Swarbrick liked Jimmy's 'hang loose' shaka celebration in Hawaii so much that he installed a wave pool in the locker room for next season. I bet he looks good doing the Heisman pose on a surfboard. Let's hear it for our golden boy with a golden arm and golden hair…Jimmy Clausen!" I took off my hat to brush my hand through my hair, yelled, "Cowabunga, dude!" and crowd surfed once again to complete the effect. My Dawgs handled me with much more care the second time around.

When the media interview round came up, everyone's favorite guest host Angela hadn't made it to campus yet. Thinking on his feet like a true Leprechaun, Juan improvised some trivia questions for all of us. The first contender he called on knew that Muffet McGraw was our women's basketball coach, but the second guy whiffed at naming our women's soccer coach. Juan mercifully gave him a second chance and luckily he knew who Mike Brey was. He got it right, but he forgot the number one rule of Leprechaun tryouts: It didn't really matter what we said so much as how we said it. When Juan asked me what year we won our first national championship in football, I came back with: "After next season we'll have twelve banners hanging in Notre Dame Stadium. The first banner will say '1924,' and the last will say '2009.' How's that sound?" My inner history nerd came out as I went a perfect three for three during the rest of our bonus trivia round.

Still no Angela, so we got the jig-off and our pushup contest out of the way. One contestant who introduced himself as Leprechaun Dave impressed me with his moxie when he took his green jacket off, rolled up his sleeves, and stretched emphatically in front of the crowd. He had swagger and I liked it. I had the highest leg kicks out of anyone during the jig though, and all fifty of my pushups came with a smile. Then Charles one-upped the rest of us by finishing his fifty with some one-armed beauties. Ladies fainted left and right.

Angela arrived just in time, cutting Charles' gun show short with a rapid-fire media interview round. When she handed me the mic, I spoke directly into the camera: "What's up, Notre Dame? This is Leprechaun Dan comin' at you live from under the Golden Dome."

She got right into it by asking me how I felt about our basketball star Luke Harangody possibly leaving school early to enter the NBA draft. I threw my full support behind the big man: "Well, Angela, I'm not sure if you've been watching Luke over the past three years, but he has become the unquestionable *beast* of the Big East. I'm excited for him, and I wish him the best of luck on his journey."

"But this is Notre Dame! Are you saying sports matter more than earning a degree here?"

"With three years' worth of a top-notch education from this University, I'm not going to question his decision-making skills, Angela." She started to get feisty after that one, throwing a vicious combo of questions about our mediocre-as-of-late football team my way. I kept my cool, emphasizing our momentum after the Hawaii Bowl and our latest recruiting efforts that successfully rescued a top prospect named Manti Te'o from the clutches of USC's evil coaching staff.

After expecting the worst, I felt relieved when my private interview with the judges ended without any intimidating interrogation tactics or questions about green beer. A legendary Notre Dame superfan named Keith served as a guest panelist, and he asked me the most important question of the interview when he invited me to comment on how I hoped fans would experience Notre Dame through me. I told him that I wanted people to remember me as a Leprechaun who gave my all for my University every time I suited up in green and gold. I wanted to inspire others, and I knew I could do so by using my relentless energy.

My interview ended at 9 p.m., and I knew the judges planned to post their decision at midnight. I prepared myself for the longest three hours of my life. Then Juan called me when I was only three pints of Guinness into my waiting party back at Alumni Hall. I lost it when I heard him say, "Hello, Mr. Leprechaun." The word "golden" kept flashing through my mind, and I danced a celebratory jig while I finished my fourth Guinness before sprinting all the way to the Joyce Center. Rather than approach with trepidation as in years past, I charged that sheet of paper with everything I had.

There it was, on an official Notre Dame letterhead: "Congratulations to the new Fighting Irish Leprechauns." My name followed immediately after in shiny gold ink. The plucky contender known as Leprechaun Dave got the Blue Leprechaun gig. I looked forward to congratulating him, but first I had a few phone calls to make. My mom came first, and I thanked her for inspiring me to dream. I left a message thanking my dad for his encouraging note, and then I called to thank Drew for drilling me in the head with that Leprechaun stuffed toy so many times when we were kids. As I went off to say a prayer of thanks at the Grotto, I received a text message from Leprechaun Matt: "Welcome to the best year of your life. Enjoy." I planned to.

For some reason I found it hard to focus during finals week. Not only did phone calls and text messages come pouring in from friends and family, but every local news source imaginable suddenly took interest in my story as well. A local South Bend news channel featured footage of seven Leprechaun hopefuls jigging arm in arm, followed by my answer to Angela's question about Luke Harangody. After the video clip she added, "Well I guess he put me in my place! That was Daniel Collins, the next Notre Dame Leprechaun!" Her words sounded like music to my ears.

Two days later, I answered a call from an unknown number and the voice on the other line sounded like it came straight from Ireland. I wasn't sure how my number made its way across the Atlantic, but I enjoyed my interview with Irish sportswriter Declan O'Kelly. When a close-up of my face appeared on IrishCentral.com, I wondered what my Irish ancestors would have thought about an article describing their descendant's plans to serve his University proudly while honoring his namesake, Daniel Collins, who emigrated from West Cork during the Great Famine.

It didn't take long for my sports-crazy city to come knocking on my door, literally. Buffalo's Channel 2 News sent a reporter to my house, and then decided to interview my mom when they couldn't get me in person. They even contacted me over Skype for their special coverage of Buffalo's first official Leprechaun. After their initial scoop, the calls came rolling in nonstop. The *Buffalo News* ran a story titled, "Lucky Leapin' Leprechaun: Nichols Grad lands Top Spot in cheering for Fighting Irish." Local sportswriter Dave Ricci compared my toughness as a Nichols football player to the Fighting Irish mentality I planned to portray as the Gold Leprechaun in a piece he wrote for the *Western New York Metro* titled, "Collins Strikes Irish Gold." The *Hamburg Sun* even went so far as to credit my education at Hamburg Middle School and Union Pleasant Elementary School as major influences that helped me land the job.

With my name generating somewhat of a buzz back home, it was only a matter of time until I got a call from Shredd and Ragan, the notorious talk show duo on Buffalo's 103.3 "The Edge" radio station. They wanted a live interview for their morning show. I got permission from our athletic department without really explaining what Shredd and Ragan were known for because I knew I could avoid their inevitable attempts at getting a controversial sound bite out of me. The segment began with our fight song playing in the background and the duo talking about how many parents in Western New York must dream of sending their children to "good ol' Irish Catholic Notre Dame." Once they got me on the line, they started off by asking if I knew how many young ladies in Irish South Buffalo had already wept with joy after hearing my exciting news. I said I knew of at least a few.

My first live radio interview went relatively well as I tried to explain the ins and outs of my new job, dispel any myths about receiving scholarship money, describe the spirit of game days at Notre Dame, and avoid any missteps. I successfully skirted the issue when they asked me if girls ever wanted to get lucky with the Leprechaun or if opposing fans ever tried to grab my lucky charms. At one point I mentioned how much I enjoyed not having to haul around a big goofy head. They asked if I meant that as smack talk directed towards foam-wearing mascots like Buffalo's very own Sabretooth. I assured them that I looked up to Sabretooth, and I only meant to criticize lesser college mascots like Michigan State's foam phony named Sparty.

The last edition of *The Observer* to come out before summer break displayed a large close-up of my face under the words "Leprechaun announced for next year: Daniel Collins plans to take role back to 'old school spirit' from Notre Dame's glory days." The article listed some quick facts next to my picture, including my favorite color (green), my favorite place on campus (Notre Dame Stadium), my favorite food in South Dining Hall (Lucky Charms), my favorite class (Irish-American History taught by Dr. Patrick Griffin), and my favorite activity (hiding gold coins around campus). When the student-reporter asked if I had a message for Fighting Irish fans in anticipation of the upcoming football season, I said they'd better get ready to embrace our return to glory.

Chapter V

Senior Year: The Golden Era

The Ten Leprechaun Commandments:

1. Thou shalt have no other team before the Fighting Irish.
2. Thou shalt not disgrace the lucky shillelagh.
3. Thou shalt maintain a high level of knowledge concerning all things Notre Dame.
4. Remember to observe game day by wearing green.
5. Honor thy predecessors by keeping thy chinstrap beard well groomed.
6. Thou shalt carry a green Sharpie at all times.
7. Thou shalt not refuse autograph requests from Fighting Irish fans.
8. Thou shalt assert superiority over Sparty whenever possible.
9. Thou shalt expect the unexpected.
10. Thou shalt not fall prey to embarrassment or intimidation.

The green and white street signs to my left and right proudly displayed big bold words written in Irish along with smaller English translations off to the side. When my lifelong friend Caitlin O'Rourke told me about her plans to volunteer at the Reilly family's fundraising event in South Buffalo I leapt at the opportunity to make my first official appearance as the Gold Leprechaun alongside some real-life fighting Irishmen and women. More than a few surprised faces turned my way when I drove up to the event in my green suit, and a series of group photos were underway before I even made it out of the parking lot. Everyone I met already knew how to strike the perfect Fighting Irish stance. No coaching necessary. It was in their blood.

Five-year-old Matthew Reilly and I prepared to sing our fight song in front of hundreds. He looked at me with an "I got this" kind of attitude when I asked if he needed any help remembering the words. The music started, I opened with the verse, and he one-upped me with a much more on key chorus. He even made up for all the notes I missed by tugging at every single heartstring. As the day went on, more and more of his family members told me how he battled spinal muscular atrophy with the same matter-of-fact courageousness he had just put on display while singing. His friends and family had formed the Spinal Muscular Atrophy Research Team (S.M.A.R.T.) as a way to fund treatment for children suffering from neuromuscular diseases. From what I saw at their event, Matthew's smile supplied his close-knit community with a constant source of inspiration.

After our big performance, Matthew and I talked a bit about Notre Dame. Then he went off to play with all the other redheaded and freckle-faced boys and girls of South Buffalo, but before he did he turned to give me a double thumbs-up. That was all I needed to see. The spirit of Notre Dame never failed to show up at events like this. I was the lucky one who got to witness it wherever I went.

Word of my first surprise Leprechaun appearance spread quickly, and the Buffalo Bisons minor league baseball team requested that I throw the ceremonial first pitch for "Irish Night" at their ballpark. I gladly accepted, though I had doubts about my pitching abilities. My limited experience at second base in Little League wasn't going to help me much, and I couldn't even remember the last time I picked up a baseball. A few days before my pitching debut, I spent the afternoon packing Big League Chew between my cheek and gum while perfecting my two-seam fastball at the sandlot down the street.

The Bisons didn't hold anything back on Irish Night. They opened the gates hours before game time for a giant tent party complete with live Irish music and several performances put on by local Irish dance academies. Spirits ran high as I posed for photos with full-grown men in kilts, little Irish dancers who could jig just about as well as they could walk, Fighting Irish fans from all over

Western New York, and hundreds more wearing the same shades of green and gold as my suit. To top it all off, the tent came fully equipped with bottomless kegs of green beer. The judges from Leprechaun tryouts would have felt right at home.

My scheduled first pitch actually turned out to be the third pitch of the evening after a pre-game presentation for Buffalo's Irishmen of the year. The honors went to New York State Assemblyman Mark Schroeder and everyone's favorite weatherman, Kevin O'Connell. Their newly customized Bisons jerseys must have psyched them out, because their throws bounced into the dirt well short of home plate. I thought, "Great, now my whole city relies on me to come through in the clutch with a save..." as I trotted out of the bullpen trying to find my inner Jonathan Papelbon. My favorite childhood mascot, Buster Bison, crouched behind the plate, signaling for a fastball. It felt good as it left my fingertips, and the Bisons shortstop told me it was the first pre-game strike he had seen all year. I gladly retired on the spot with my perfect save percentage still intact.

My theory held true when I joined Buster for his ritual t-shirt toss between innings: Neither the sport nor the city mattered, without fail people went absolutely nuts for free shirts. Buster and I discussed this fundamental fact of life while he labored to take off his huge foam head backstage, where we had ourselves a mascot moment. He told me about his standard practice of picking one lucky kid to race him around the bases after every seventh-inning stretch, and how the promotions staff never let him win. He had paid his dues, and all he wanted in life was one well-deserved moment of glory. I couldn't let Buster down. After all, he signed a brand new ball cap for me on my eleventh birthday.

I agreed to throw the match on one condition: I couldn't let Buster look faster than me. I had a reputation to uphold, so we came up with the perfect plan. As I rounded third base on my way home, Buster's trusty sidekick Buffalo Chip blocked my path with his fists raised Fighting Irish style. Buster slid into home as thousands of suddenly interested fans watched me pummel Chip. I felt like Russell Crowe in *Gladiator* until the announcer called out, "Wow, it looks like Buster just won his first race ever! Sorry folks, but I guess the luck of the Irish just ran out."

Autograph requests came pouring in after the footage of my staged fight with Chip hit the air, and my mom found herself unofficially employed as my publicity agent for the summer. I did my best to answer the rising demand while saving myself for the long football season ahead. When the president of the Notre Dame Club of Buffalo called, I decided to make one final appearance before returning to campus. My assignment: surprise the crowd by popping up on stage while the Notre Dame Glee Club sang our fight song as the grand finale of their concert at a local church. I arrived just seconds before the first intermission, so they ushered me into a side room where I hid to avoid causing a scene. While waiting to hear the words "Rally sons of Notre Dame…" I met an ancient-looking priest who asked, "Are those your real ears?" That was a first. My naturally rosy cheeks usually led to questions about my use of makeup, but I never considered my ears elflike enough to draw such speculation.

I began to wonder if the Glee Club had forgotten about me as the concert continued and an alum brought his four-year-old twins in to meet me. Apparently he had unwisely alerted them of my presence during the intermission, and they had grown restless to the point of tears in anticipation of my appearance. They walked through the door wide-eyed and clinging to their dad's pant legs. Nothing I tried could break their trance. They simply stared in utter disbelief as if they had just caught Santa Claus sliding down their chimney. None of my questions reached them, and they continued to stare directly at me rather than at their dad's camera when I knelt down with my fists raised for a photo. Then, just as their dad ushered them away, the little boy turned back towards me to yell "Go Irish!" with an authoritative fist pump. His sister giggled and they both ran off bashfully. Impressed by his last-ditch effort to avow his loyalty to Notre Dame, I pointed in his direction as I ran out onto the stage. He hid behind his dad once again, peering out at me while I got the whole church chanting "WE ARE ND!" We all linked arms in a big circle, and the Glee Club led us in the Alma Mater.

When I got word that legendary Fighting Irish head coach Lou Holtz would be among the inductees honored at the

2009 College Football Hall of Fame Enshrinement Grand Parade in South Bend, I flew back to campus a few weeks early on my own dime. I couldn't miss this once-in-a-lifetime chance to honor one of the most influential men in the history of Notre Dame. The parade included over a hundred separate units of cheerleaders, mascots, marching bands, antique cars, and floats for each inductee. I made my way to the back of the long line towards Lou's very own Notre Dame fire truck, stopping to honor photo requests from beauty queens and NFL cheerleaders along the way. Just before the parade got moving I hopped up onto the fire truck to tell Lou how much I enjoyed reading his autobiography. He responded with, "Thanks. I like your green tie. It's very sharp. Life is all about choices. Make good choices, like that tie there, and you'll do well in life."

We set off through downtown South Bend, chanting "Lou! Lou! Lou!" to the tune of Tchaikovsky's *1812 Overture* for over an hour straight. I must have handed out over five hundred high-fives while constantly scurrying back and forth to both sides of the street as Lou's fire truck followed closely behind. He thanked us for the escort when we finally reached the enshrinement festival outside the College Football Hall of Fame, where we spent the rest of the day posing for photos with fans. Brutus the Ohio State Buckeye, Willie the Northwestern Wildcat, and the nameless Valparaiso Crusader joined me in leading the inductees onto the stage, where we all worked together to get the fans on their feet. After a little coaxing from the crowd, I couldn't help but assert myself as the self-proclaimed King of College Mascots by beating them all in a 40-yard dash. I even agreed to run backwards just to make it fair, but they never stood a chance as I effortlessly chalked up a win for foamless mascots everywhere.

Back in South Bend, with only weeks to go until cheer camp, I set to work researching anything and everything I needed to know in order to become the most knowledgeable Leprechaun Notre Dame had ever seen. I felt the need to make up for a childhood spent living in total ignorance of the Fighting Irish, so I took several trips to the university archives to brush up on my sports history. I knew that a large part of any Leprechaun's success involved the ability to engage fans with well-informed discourse, so I studied the storied past of our football team in addition to much more recent happenings. The dedicated diehards writing about Notre Dame for websites like "Her Loyal Sons," "UHND.com," "Bleacher Report," and "The Blue-Gray Sky" became my go-to sources of information when it came to current events. To gain a better understanding of our nearly unfathomable ocean of tradition without getting overwhelmed by its enormity, I chose seven lucky books that promised to turn me into an expert on all things Notre Dame:

The Spirit of Notre Dame by Jim Langford;

Shake Down the Thunder: The Creation of Notre Dame Football by Murray Sperber;

Loyal Sons: The Story of the Four Horsemen and Notre Dame Football's 1924 Champions by Jim Lefebvre;

Forgotten Four: Notre Dame's Greatest Backfield and the 1953 Undefeated Season by Donald J. Hubbard and Mark O. Hubbard;

Talking Irish: The Oral History of Notre Dame Football by Steve Delsohn;

For Notre Dame Fans Only: The New Saturday Bible by Rich Wolfe;

May I Have Your Attention Please: Wit and Wisdom from the N.D. Pressbox by Mike Collins and Sgt. Tim McCarthy

A strict regimen of fifty pushups between each chapter ensured that I would be able to keep up with our offense in the fall when Jimmy Clausen started lighting up the scoreboard over Notre Dame Stadium. I dreamt about cranking out at least fifty every game while I poured over my self-assigned reading list.

My preseason study habits supplemented the research I had already begun under the direction of Dr. Patrick Griffin for my senior thesis titled "Reviving the Fighting Irish: The real significance of the words 'Fighting Irish' at Notre Dame." In the process of discerning the meaning behind the nickname I intended to personify, I read a great deal about the mind-boggling lives of Fr. Edward Sorin, the French priest belonging to the Congregation of Holy Cross who founded Notre Dame in 1842, and Knute Rockne, the greatest football coach of all time. No one other than Fr. Theodore Hesburgh had accomplished more to shape the spirit of Notre Dame than Sorin and Rockne. Both were men of steadfast faith and determination, unafraid to act on their own convictions in order to realize their unshakable goals. Both men also exhibited somewhat stubborn and delusional behavior at times, which wasn't necessarily a bad thing. As movers of many, they generated inspiration that set the stage for our future glory at Notre Dame. With their stories firmly planted in my head as I approached my one defining year as the Gold Leprechaun, I vowed to adopt a Sorin-esque, Rockne-like "Fighting Irish" mentality when it came to leaving behind a legacy I could be proud of.

My newfound determination and my authentically Irish attitude came into play when I set in motion a plan to revive our pep rallies for the 2009 football season. I spent the previous summer exploring Ireland with my good friend Grant Schmidt, who now happened to be the student body president. Reunited by our quest to give all that we could to Notre Dame, we made it our combined goal to bring the collective voice of the students in front of the powers that be. Our classmates had grown restless with the administration's approach to pep rallies over the past several years, and a season-long boycott loomed in the future. They wanted less Disney World and more war rally. The administration wanted a family friendly atmosphere. Grant and I walked into the Golden Dome to negotiate a compromise.

We reached a deal that made both sides relatively happy, with the first pep rally set to kick off our highly anticipated season alongside Dillon Hall's signature event on South Quad. The administration insisted that the rest of our rallies follow detailed scripts from a new location in a park on the outskirts of campus known as the Irish Green. In return, they agreed to let us host an unscripted student-only sendoff rally on campus in the Stepan Center prior to our road game against the Michigan Skunkbears. Though we didn't exactly have the leverage we needed to get anything in writing, we secured tentative promises to host the rally leading up to our rivalry game against the Southern Cal Trojans in Notre Dame Stadium, as well as our final rally on senior night in the Joyce Center.

Satisfied with a deal we could bring back to our constituents, we came up with a way to spin our compromise as a resounding win. Grant crafted a sincere letter in which he artfully conveyed his genuine love for his University, his best wishes for his fellow students, and his deep respect for the administration. I wrote the first of many letters that I planned as part of my campaign to elevate the Leprechaun position to a new level through my active use of social media, open dialogue with the student body, writing letters to *The Observer*, and becoming a more visible campus figure in general. I hoped that my efforts would unify our students, alums, fans, and administration in order to breathe life back into the spirit of Notre Dame. My first message to the entire student body included the following:

> Calling all true Fighting Irish fans,
>
> This place is magical. Why? The storied tradition,

the worldwide fame, the unparalleled atmosphere, the collective commitment to excellence, the transformation that takes place on campus every game day, the incredibly successful sports programs that continue to impress while upholding the highest levels of academic integrity, the really, really, ridiculously good-looking Leprechauns, and the pride we all take in knowing that no other university in the world can compare to our beloved Notre Dame. But what's the single most important force behind the magic that fills this place? What makes it all possible year after year? *The Students*. As Domers we carry that magic on our shoulders, building it up and passing it on to those who will join our family in the future.

So I ask you, *the students*, to please save our pep rallies. It's up to you, and only you can make it happen. Do so by showing up in record numbers and making it *your* show. Get loud, stay loud, and don't stop. Every Friday as we prepare to take part in the greatest of all traditions on the most sacred of all football fields, we must come together as a student body to share in that magic.

For Notre Dame,
Your Fightin' Irish Leprechaun

Cheer camp in the charming old-school gym at the end of South Quad known as "The Rock" consisted of big guys learning how to throw small girls around for a whole week straight, with the occasional human pyramid including one of the Leprechauns. Other than rubbing Rockne's bronze nose for good luck at least three times a day and making sure to supplement my diet with plenty of minerals from the drinking fountains that tasted like blood, I spent most of my time at cheer camp daydreaming. I dreamed about my last year living in the Dawg House and I dreamed about delivering fiery warlike speeches to crowds of thousands, but most of my thoughts focused on Notre Dame Football. The upcoming season dominated my mind so completely that I began to play out each game on our schedule over and over in my head.

I knew our team would ride the wave of momentum left over from the Hawaii Bowl to an easy victory in our home opener against Nevada, especially considering the atmosphere I intended to create on opening weekend. Week two against the Skunkbears would give us a test, but the first student-only sendoff rally in the modern era of Notre Dame Football couldn't fail to bring us a win. If Michigan State showed up for week three looking anything like their shoddy mascot, we would make them pay for planting their flag into our field two years earlier. After starting out with a 3-0 record, it would only take a quick road trip to put the nerds over at Purdue in their place during week four. Then we basically had week five off with little more than a scrimmage against a Washington team that went 0-12 the year before.

Then came Southern Cal. Week six would define my time as the Gold Leprechaun, and I planned to do everything in my power to make sure we gave the Trojans a rude awakening when they stepped onto our campus. I wanted that Jeweled Shillelagh. I wanted it bad. If we could pull off a David versus Goliath stunt against Southern Cal, we wouldn't even have to blink against Boston College, Washington State, Navy, Pittsburgh, Connecticut, or Stanford as we set our sights on a national championship. These were the thoughts swirling through my head as I prepared to spend the next several months making the Notre Dame Family believe again. The cheerleaders called me delusional, but I was only trying to follow in the footsteps of Sorin and Rockne.

Camp concluded with Sunday Mass in the historic log chapel nestled away in a picturesque corner of our campus next to St. Mary's Lake, where it all began for Fr. Sorin. I sat down in the first creaky wooden pew to reflect on how far our small Catholic school had come since he founded it in 1842, and how his vision had created such a powerful force for good in this world. Everyone in that chapel had been blessed with the opportunity to live within that power. We were all about to spend one Golden year of our lives representing it in front of Fighting Irish fans around the world. During Mass, our priest explained how the Holy Spirit exists as the sense of joy that becomes love when shared. He told us that spreading joy and sharing love had become our vocation. I thought about how much better his description of our duties sounded than the typical nine-to-five. During the moment of silence after his homily, I asked Notre Dame our Mother to pray for us and guide me as I set out to change the world in my own small way.

Christmas came in August when we returned to our team hotel to find several industrial-size garbage bags filled with more Adidas gear than we could ever wear. Anyone who saw us would have thought they just walked onto the set for a commercial shoot when we congregated in the conference room for some team bonding exercises. We all sat cross-legged in a big circle on the floor, telling our favorite stories from the summer one at a time. Story time became show-and-tell when my turn came and I unveiled the fresh Leprechaun tattoo on my right bicep. My new ink flew in the face of our conservative team policy just a bit, so the gasps and white faces I caused didn't surprise me much.

The story I told went like this: Between my first official Gold Leprechaun appearances back home in Buffalo, I decided to take a day trip to Niagara Falls where a well-renowned tattoo artist named John-Paul Calderon waited to put a permanent Leprechaun logo on my arm. I had been planning to go through with it ever since I got the Golden gig, and my mom even agreed to come with me as long as she could use her nursing expertise to make sure the whole process stayed sterile. The crew at Niagara Street Tattoo couldn't stop laughing when they found out I brought my mom along for my first tat. Situated nicely between two boarded-up buildings on a blighted street, their shop appeared straight out of a documentary about the seedy urban underground. I loved the authenticity of the whole experience. John-Paul even joked that I was smart to park my Jeep where I could see it in case I had to interrupt his work in order to prevent the locals from engaging in some grand theft auto.

My new little Irish friend took almost two hours to appear in full color on my arm. The owner of the shop called a reporter from the *Niagara Gazette,* who interviewed John-Paul and me for an article he planned to write about my tattoo. I told him how my new badge of honor would remind me that every time I suited up in green I represented my Irish heritage as well as my University. John-Paul worked meticulously to the tune of his favorite Naughty By Nature album, only stopping to say, "I can tell how stoked this dude is to get himself tattooed on his arm, so I'm gonna make this shit look like a sticker!" That he did. When I first showed it to my friends on the football team, John Ryan pinned me down with his 6'5" frame to rub it off with a wet paper towel. He finally gave up when the Leprechaun refused to fade despite the rest of my arm turning bright red.

☘

A rainbow stretched across the sky when I stepped out of Alumni Hall on the way to my first on-campus appearance as the Gold Leprechaun. I hoped it stood as a sign of good things to come for the Fighting Irish. The big Windsor knot in my tie and the fresh custom Kelly green Adidas high tops on my feet drew several compliments as I stopped for photos with fans along the route to the Joyce Center. When I arrived, the frosh-o pep rally had already gotten underway. I could hear the familiar voice of my friend Grant Schmidt welcoming our freshmen home.

The collective liveliness of so many new students brought a tangible sense of energy into the arena. My butterflies came back as I waited for my cue to make a grand entrance, and I felt the same rush I experienced three years before when the band came marching in to the brass blast of our fight song. I wanted to stir that same emotion in the unknown future Leprechaun who sat somewhere within that crowd of freshmen, so I quoted Leprechaun Kevin's immortal words when I went onstage to welcome them all into our Notre Dame Family.

The cheerleaders and I spent the next morning teaching our cheers to the new crop of freshmen at each dorm. I took the opportunity to let them know how blessed they were to be part of a tradition unlike anything else in the world. Countless students their age would have given anything to be freshmen at Notre Dame, so I told them to earn the privileged position they held by embracing the spirit of this place. I also guaranteed they would lose the beat by going way too fast the first time we sang our fight song together. Every year without fail, the overly excited freshmen clapped at a faster and faster pace until they finished well ahead of everyone else. This year was no different. My warnings didn't help them one bit, but they made up for their lack of rhythm with plenty of enthusiasm.

After feasting on peppered flank steak at South Dining Hall, we visited the Hannah & Friends Neighborhood, a charity organization head football coach Charlie Weis created as a tribute to his daughter with special needs. We saw another side of Coach Weis that afternoon as he patiently interacted with all the guests who depended on Hannah & Friends for their quality of life. After starting a few cheers and performing some stunts with the cheerleaders, I enjoyed meeting all of the sincerely compassionate staff members and genuinely happy guests. We talked about football, shared laughs, and played tag with the kids. Before we left I asked the in-house balloon-animal specialist if he knew how to make a Leprechaun. Without hesitation he threw together a remarkably accurate likeness of me. He was ecstatic when I gladly agreed to pose for a photo while holding his masterpiece—another small moment to remind me just how easily simple acts of kindness could make a big difference. God, I loved my job.

When I got back to Alumni Hall I found all of our freshmen in the chapel listening to our hall staff paraphrase the endless catalogue of rules contained within our dreaded student handbook called *Du Lac*. They looked way too somber, so I lightened the mood by popping in to tell them about the tradition by which every Dawg would jump around screaming as loudly as possible whenever anyone uttered the word "Alumni" at a pep rally. They promised they would honor the tradition, so I agreed to insert the magic word into as many of my speeches as possible. Before I left them to tend to their more serious matters, I made sure to reinforce the fact that Father George Rozum would go down in history as the most beloved rector of all time. The sense of community he fostered within the hallowed halls of the Dawg House year after year could not be matched, and I looked forward to sharing that bond with my new group of brothers.

My first game as the Gold Leprechaun featured a Saturday night matchup between our unranked women's volleyball team and #5 Stanford. On my way, I came across a wedding party taking photos between Notre Dame Stadium and Touchdown Jesus. I always loved how often I found tourists and fans aiming their cameras at all the iconic sights on our campus. It reminded me that I went to school in the middle of a highly sought after vacation destination. When the groomsmen saw me approaching they started humming the fight song, so I knew I had to make a quick detour. Little did I know they would reshoot their entire series of wedding pictures just so they could feature me front and center. The photographer made sure to snap several shots of everyone imitating Touchdown Jesus' outstretched arms, more of just the groom and me squaring off in matching Leprechaun poses, and one of me carrying the bride in my arms honeymoon style. The groom didn't even seem to mind that last one. In fact, he told me that I just made his whole weekend. Once he noticed the death stare coming from his soon-to-be bride, he qualified his statement with a wink.

We already led Stanford by a game when I made it onto the court. The cheerleaders looked perturbed, but they eventually agreed that I had a pretty good excuse for arriving late. Members of every Notre Dame team from football to fencing filled the stands for what was the first athletic contest of the year in any sport. I wondered if that type of unity existed at other schools. The rest of the fans marveled at what they saw, and their audible buzz grew louder every time another well-known football player walked in. After our girls won the second game, the entire men's swim team stood up, ripped off their track suits, and threw each other in the air for twenty-five pushups while wearing nothing but their blue and gold Speedos. The sight must have added extra motivation to get out of there as soon as possible, because Stanford went down without a fight in the final game. Either that, or my game-time decision to throw hot dogs when we ran out of t-shirts gave our crowd the added incentive they needed to cheer us onward to victory. I was never very accurate while throwing t-shirts, but I had deadly accuracy with a hot dog. I was downright surgical with those things, tossing them straight into the hands of my chosen targets. Even Jimmy Clausen looked impressed.

Inspired by the spirit I witnessed at the volleyball game, I did my best wartime propaganda impression in another open letter to the student body. Part of it appeared in *The Observer* on the first day of classes:

> Attention Notre Dame,
>
> Your nation needs you. Football season is upon us, and we will soon add a new chapter to the greatest tradition in all of sports. The outcome of that chapter rests in your hands. A great opportunity stands before us, and we all must heed the battle call. What will *you* do for Notre Dame this season?
>
> Freshmen: Take it all in and embrace the glory of your first game because you will remember it for

the rest of your life. Seniors: This is your last chance to leave a legacy. Alumni: Don't shy away from showing your support. After all, you were once students too.

For glory, for honor, for Notre Dame, Your Fightin' Irish Leprechaun.

Week One
#23 Notre Dame Fighting Irish
vs.
Nevada Wolf Pack

Notre Dame Stadium
Notre Dame, IN

My dad has three older sisters and nine older brothers. I have a lot of cousins. About thirty of them made the trek to Notre Dame for my first football weekend as the Gold Leprechaun. So did most of my closest friends from back home, including Drew and his fanatical cousin Mitch. A block of seventy tickets inside Notre Dame Stadium belonged to the Collins family, and everyone pitched in to rent a tent in the VIP tailgate area for game day. My cousin Lauren, now married to none other than my original source of inspiration, Jimmy Ryan, made a bulk order of Kelly green t-shirts that read: "Leprechaun Dan's #1 Fans."

I noticed a peculiar energy building on campus all week. It reminded me of something I felt before, but I couldn't quite place it. Then, while ceremoniously carving my initials into the lucky shillelagh like every Leprechaun before me, I suddenly knew what it was. The last time that type of electric feel hit campus, I was a freshman and Brady Quinn was set to lead the #3 Fighting Irish on a national championship run. As the weekend drew near, the impression became more recognizable. The students, players, coaches, and fans were finally starting to believe again. I sensed it. Notre Dame was back.

The promotions staff came disdainfully close to completely cutting me out of my first pep rally. They wanted to hand the reins over to the residents of Dillon Hall, who had planned several skits and speeches but certainly never paid their dues through three straight attempts at tryouts and a full year as the Blue Leprechaun. Always willing to negotiate a compromise, I convinced them to let me set the stage with a pre-rally speech. That way I could show off my skills as a silver-tongued orator to my seventy-plus friends and family members who drove hours to see me without trampling on Dillon's dainty dignity.

Little did they know that my Dawgs and I had already set in motion a prank for the ages. My friends walked right into Dillon Hall incognito wearing red Dillonite t-shirts and carrying a hefty roll of fabric. They told anyone who asked that it read: "Alumni Hall sucks!" I secretly gave the signal by saying, "Mic check...one...two," and at that moment they unfurled the banner from a window on the third floor in front of 10,000 fans just as the pep rally started streaming live on UND.com. The bright green letters spray-painted across several white sheets spelled out: "Suck it Dillon! Go Dawgs Go!"

Pretending I had nothing to do with the distraction taking place behind me, I addressed the largest crowd I had ever spoken to with a theatrical drawn out "Notre Daaame! Make...some...noooise!" I was pretty sure I just caused South Quad to register on the Richter scale.

"Who's ready to watch our Fightin' Irish hunt down the Nevada Wolf Pack tomorrow?" Another earthquake ensued. I really wanted to go with the "Who's afraid of the Big Bad Wolf?" routine I had planned out, but I switched to my alternate speech when the promotions staff refused to let me bring an actual skinned wolf hide onstage.

"It's officially football season! I said make some *noise*!" Thousands of students wearing their respective dorm colors gathered closer to the stage while starting a "Here come the Irish!" chant on their own. I let them take over until they ran out of steam.

"It's good to be back. I can feel it in the air. Every time I walk past our stadium...every time I look up at our Golden Dome...and every time I hear our marching band play our fight song...*chills* run up and down my spine. It's a feeling I only get here at Notre Dame. How many of you know just what I'm talkin' about?" By their response, it sounded like most of them knew exactly what I was talking about.

"If you don't feel it yet, you will tomorrow. If you don't feel it then, you might need to check in over at our health services building because you don't have a pulse." My first attempt at a joke in front of thousands didn't flop. I liked where this was headed.

"Before we get started, I just wanna give a few shout-outs real quick to my friends and family, rollin' over seventy deep right now, most of them all the way from Buffalo. Hey everyone! I love you, mom!" A resounding "Awww!" came from the residents of every women's dorm on campus, plus St. Mary's.

"Just to make sure you're ready for our football team to come out here, I want to hear a loud Fightin' Irish battle cry from all you students. Lemme hear ya!" A "WE ARE ND!" chant sprung up instantaneously.

"Now how 'bout the newest members of our Notre Dame Family. Let's hear it from all you freshmen!" A slightly quieter, much faster "We are ND!" chant followed.

"Now all the lovely ladies of Notre Dame and St. Mary's...Yell out your phone numbers on the count of three. Ready?" My second joke didn't flop either, but the promotions staff looked like they wanted to yank the cord from my mic. I picked up the pace, but not before one final shout-out for my brothers in Alumni Hall.

"Now let's kick it back to those glory days all you old-time Domers always brag about. Let's hear it from all the Alumni!" At the sound of our magic word, my Kelly-green-clad Dawgs barked, woofed, howled, snarled, and screamed until I finally got them to stop.

"Sorry, folks. They're a bunch of wild animals. Just let me leave you with one final message, because tomorrow the Nevada Wolf Pack is coming to Notre Dame Stadium for the first time ever. All the critics love talking about their star quarterback Colin Kaepernick's amazing pistol offense. Well, I'm not really sure about that. But I do know whatever kind of pistol he's packin' is gonna look like a kid's cap gun next to the full arsenal of heavy weaponry our offense plans to drop on his team tomorrow. You know why? Because we are...Notre Dame." One final "WE ARE ND!" chant served as a fitting welcome to our football players, who arrived onstage with perfect timing.

Dinner at Rocco's that night gave me a chance to carbo-load for game day. I signed an 8 x 10 for the owner Warren, making sure to include my ringing endorsement for the best pizza in the Midwest. After walking over to the midnight drum circle on the steps of the Golden Dome with a posse that would've put the Beastie Boys to shame, I decided to call it a night. As much as I wanted to celebrate our upcoming victory with my friends and family, I knew I had a long day ahead of me in the ninety-degree heat.

Game day began at 8 a.m. with Metallica's hardcore version of the Irish classic "Whiskey in the Jar" blasting from my alarm clock—my kind of wake-up call. I suited up while listening to some of my favorite Irish rock ballads from Flogging Molly, Dropkick Murphys, The Tossers, The Pogues, The Young Dubliners, and Shilelagh Law mixed in with tracks from the Band of the Fighting Irish. The cheerleaders assembled behind Alumni Hall at 9 a.m., and our marathon meet-and-greet tour got underway.

Our first stop included a cheer or two, a few words from yours truly, and a photo opp for the Sorin Society tailgate outside the Morris Inn. Then we wasted no time making our way over to the Irish Green, where I said a few more words to the field full of fans trying to suck down their snow cones before they melted in the heavy heat. They weren't the most receptive group, but I fought for their attention by telling them how important their duties as fans were to the success of our football team. I always brought the same energy to every appearance, knowing that even if I reached only one person I could still end up having a profound impact somewhere down the line. Inspiration had come to me that way in the past, so I tried to pay it forward whenever I got a chance.

If the veteran cheerleaders expected to mingle casually with the posh fans in the VIP area, my family made sure to break them out of their regular routine. My little cousins swarmed us like bees around a hive. I gathered them together for their own private, mini pep rally: "Come on, Collins Clan, its opening day at Notre Dame!" My dad cheered louder than everyone else combined.

"I've been waiting for this day since last Christmas Eve when Santa landed in the Hawaiian Islands just a couple hours early to deliver the greatest present any Notre Dame fan could ever ask for. With that elusive bowl victory behind us, our team looks forward to riding high on their wave of momentum all season long. Now it's up to us to make sure they stay on top of that wave. When you get inside Notre Dame Stadium I want you to let everyone know the Collins family came to cheer us onward to victory!" Based on their reaction, the fans in neighboring tents probably thought Mel Gibson just gave his *Braveheart* speech next door. Once all the little ones stopped running around and screaming, we took a Fightin' Irish family portrait. I wished I could have stayed, but I had plenty more fans to pump up before kickoff.

Three more mini pep rallies with three more versions of the same speech followed as we made our way through the tailgate-filled parking lots into the Joyce Center. After performing for the former varsity-letter winners and their families inside the Monogram Club, we devoured their buffet. Recharged from a little down time in the air-conditioning away from the steamy sea of people outside, we jogged to the Nieuwland Science Center while chanting "Gooo Irish! Beeeat Wolf Pack!" the whole way. Our strategy for avoiding long delays without insulting anyone worked. If we needed to get somewhere on campus without fans stopping us for photos, we just had to run so they couldn't keep up and cheer loudly so we couldn't hear them.

I led the cheerleaders in a Hail Mary before we ran through LaFortune Student Center, much to the surprise of the hungry fans waiting patiently in the serpentine Subway line coiled around the concourse. More fans mobbed us for the remainder of the fifteen minutes we had left until the Band of the Fighting Irish signaled the start of its Step-Off Parade from the Golden Dome to Notre Dame Stadium. Our venerated drum major, Aaron Hernandez, blew his whistle, raised his ornate golden scepter, and away we went.

The crowds formed a human tunnel along both edges of the sidewalk all the way across campus. I led the way with all twelve Gold Squad Cheerleaders, followed by the Irish Guard. As the officially recognized protectors of our band, the Guardsmen marched with purpose. I remembered hearing that an Indiana state law gave them permission to forcibly remove any person impeding their progress on game day. I wasn't about to test whether a Leprechaun qualified as a person, so I did my best to high-five every outstretched arm without lagging behind too much.

When we got to the road encircling Notre Dame Stadium, a flock of former cheerleaders and Leprechauns broke through the wall of people to deliver flying chest bumps to their protégés. My adrenaline-assisted airtime almost landed Leprechaun emeritus Juan in the hospital. The male cheerleaders formed a circle around me on the road directly south of Touchdown Jesus, I did a break down, and we all high-stepped our way into Notre Dame Stadium with thousands upon thousands of fans cheering us on. The temperature skyrocketed to over a hundred degrees when the entire marching band packed into the tunnel behind us. Someone handed me two plastic water bottles, both of which I emptied in a matter of seconds. I laughed at the salty sweat stains already expanding across my green suit as I stood in the shade—winded, worn out, and smiling.

☘

We walked through the main tunnel into an already-packed house, with the student section filling up at a steady pace. My seventy friends and family members stood out in the upper bowl with their matching green t-shirts, so I acknowledged them with a wave. My most important pre-game task involved assembling the giant steel flagpole covered with fresh flakes of the same 24-karat gold that the managers used to paint the football helmets. I hooked it up to the monster blue and gold flag made from the same material as our team's football jerseys, which I rolled up tightly before tucking it away in a safe place. The NBC cameras caught me practicing my push-ups, so I called Charles over to reinforce my gun show with some artillery. Before I knew it, less than five minutes remained on the pre-game countdown clock—time to get in position for my big moment with the flag. Just then, Jerome Bettis and Tim Brown walked by. I casually said hello to my two favorite NFL players of all time. Only at Notre Dame.

"Go when the gold helmets hit the sun!" That's what the NBC cameraman yelled my way when he got in position to capture the football team in the tunnel. My flag might as well have been a red cape. Our hulking linebacker Brian Smith stood in front of his teammates, all of them ready to charge. For some reason his lethal gaze focused directly on me. Then I realized at the most inopportune moment that I definitely couldn't outrun any of the freakishly athletic specimens waiting to sprint through that tunnel. After another Hail Mary to calm my nerves, I resorted to repeating, "Don't trip…Don't trip…" over and over.

The gold helmets hit the sun. I took off. My flag unfurled with a snap. Slow motion. My feet left the ground. They didn't come back down. I watched as 81,000 stood to scream. They lifted me…Higher and higher…Euphoria. I didn't come back down. One hundred yards passed beneath me. I thought I felt Heaven. Then I thought, "Maybe this is Heaven!" It would have made for a good death—straight into College Football Heaven.

Not even two minutes ticked off the game clock before a bucketful of pure glorious sweat soaked all the way through my many layers of authentic Leprechaun garb. My Kelly green coattails took on a much darker shade. I went all out from the very first "Gooo Irish!" of the opening kick until the final "WE ARE ND!" before halftime. Always the responsible pre-med major, Mike left his cheerleading post to shower me with an ice-cold bottle of water. He probably saved my life. All that jigging, stunting, and shillelagh waving at midfield left me feeling five pounds lighter as I limped up the tunnel to escape the punishing sun for a while.

Jimmy Clausen couldn't have picked a better target for the first touchdown of 2009. Kyle Rudolph played like a champion every day, both on and off the field. I loved that I got to smack his shoulder pads and tap the top of his gold helmet when he hauled in Jimmy's bullet over the middle to make the score 6-0, but I loved the energy our whole team responded with even more. Our previously suspect defense came out swinging, led by stalwart linebacker Toryan Smith. The Wolf Pack didn't earn a single first down during any of their first three possessions. Even young Manti Te'o saw his first action as a freshman, taking down superstar Colin Kaepernick for the first official tackle of his career. We had it in the bag by halftime. Nevada's big foam puppy dog mascots Alphie and Wolfie Jr. admitted they were just happy to be there when I met them in the tunnel before heading back out for the second half.

The game ended with fans whispering about Jimmy Clausen as a Heisman hopeful after his 300 yards and four touchdowns. The play of the game belonged to Michael Floyd, though. He took a quick swing pass all the way to the house for 88 of his 189 total yards, capping off a three-touchdown day. With a view most sports fans would kill for, I watched him run all 88 of those yards directly at me as he galloped down the sideline like a stallion. The front page of *The Observer* called our 35-0 shutout victory an "Opening Statement." I felt like I could definitely get used to this line of work.

Week Two
#18 Notre Dame Fighting Irish
vs.
Michigan Skunkbears
The Big House
Ann Arbor, MI

Grant Schmidt and I masterminded a back-to-basics old-school throwback grungy, sweaty, grimy, raucous rally our classmates would never forget. No videos, no scripts, no long list of guest speakers and, most important, no authority figures—just the team, the band, and the students packed into that leaky half of a giant golf ball they called the Stepan Center. The way it was meant to be. I wrote another open letter to the entire student body:

> Domers,
>
> Our football game this weekend marks the continuation of an epic rivalry. Your brothers in Blue and Gold are currently preparing to take the field in Ann Arbor in order to defend your honor against the lowly stinking Skunkbears of Michigan. They cannot do this alone. Each one of you has a role to play.
>
> A *student-only* "Sendoff Rally" will take place in Stepan Center on Thursday night. This rally will signal our return to the old-school spirit from a time when students packed together into the field house

> like sardines to shake down the thunder while throwing effigies of opposing players and coaches through the air. This is our chance to wake up those echoes by coming out in full force.
>
> Help your team recapture that glory. The doors open at 7:30. *Students only.*
>
> For Notre Dame,
> Your Fightin' Irish Leprechaun

The Blessed Men and Brothers of Alumni Hall received a separate note letting them in on the secret instructions given to me by the head of game-day security. A Domer himself, he looked forward to watching us attempt to re-create the spirit of his glory days. He told me off the record that his staff would turn a blind eye to any items students happened to sneak into the rally. I encouraged my Dawgs to unload the toilet paper from every bathroom stall in the dorm. My promise to stage-dive into their midst provided extra incentive to show up front and center.

I paced back and forth behind Stepan Center as dusk set in Thursday night, hoping at least a couple hundred students would choose our rally over pregaming Club Fever. They didn't exactly pack the house, but the thousand or so diehards who did come made up for their classmates' lack of spirit with war paint, Irish flags, and enough toilet paper to blanket the whole state of Indiana.

Grant gave the signal by yelling "Go Irish!" over the mic, and I came running in with the cheerleaders, pom squad, Irish Guard, and marching band right behind me. After jumping onstage, I held up an old #21 Desmond Howard Michigan jersey. With the whole crowd booing and throwing toilet paper at me, I slowly tore it in half, tossing the tattered pieces to the angry mob below.

"Notre Daaame! Wow! Look at you! You've been askin' for a rally like this ever since I can remember. Guess what! We finally did it!" The students voiced their approval.

"You've also probably heard about plans to tear this hideous building down ever since you can remember. Guess what! Tonight's our chance! Let's tear this mother *down*!" They almost did. Oddly enough, the head of security looked pleased.

"Our team is out there waiting to come in for an old-school sendoff like they used to have back in the days of yore. So let's welcome them with the precursor to our "Here come the Irish!" chant. We'll start with the ladies, then the guys will echo, and we'll go back and forth real slow. Ready? Take it away, ladies!"

The team bobbed their heads to the unfamiliar cadence while they walked through the crowd up onto the stage. They liked it. Once they all crowded onto the much-too-small platform, I signaled for the band to blast out our fight song: "Scholars, athletes, ladies, and gentlemen…please join me in welcoming *your* 2009 Fightin' Irish football team!"

The NCAA had reprimanded Michigan before the season even began because they went well beyond the hourly limit each team must follow for mandatory practices. I hoped my highly intelligent classmates would pick up on my subtle jab at their program as I introduced our first speaker Brian Smith:

"Wow... If those Skunkbears up in Ann Arbor could see us right now, they'd be pretty damn scared. Actually... after what we did to them last year, I'm pretty sure they're already scared. Our first speaker tonight has a lot to do with that fear after taking a fumble 35 yards to the house last time they stepped inside Notre Dame Stadium. I hear they've been putting in a lot of hours trying to figure out a way to stop this guy. No, really...They've been putting in *a lot* of hours...but not even a little extra practice can help them. He's simply unstoppable. You saw him take down Colin Kaepernick with that vicious sack last week. Give it up for Brian Smith!"

Brian didn't want to give up the mic. That was okay. The crowd loved the story he told about how his dad, a fullback for the Fighting Irish back in the early 1980s, refused to buy him any Skunkbear swag as a kid. For some reason, Brian happened to like their colors when he was young, but his dad sat him down to tell him that no son of his would ever wear a Michigan jersey. His ten-minute epic tale probably would've gone on much longer if it weren't for the frenzied chant he incited. With no adults around to scold them, the students felt free enough to belt out "Muck 'em up! Muck 'em up! Michigan Sucks!" Except they didn't say "muck."

Brian finally gave up when the somewhat vulgar chant grew so loud he couldn't even hear himself over the mic.

He handed it back to me laughing, so I began my next introduction: "I'm no fan of statistics, but I think we all need to take a moment to ponder the insane numbers our next speaker put up last weekend. I'm talkin' crazy, stupid video-game numbers. Three of his four catches went for touchdowns. Really? Hey, Mike! Why couldn't you break free on that last one to go a perfect four for four?"

Michael Floyd laughed as he grabbed two mics, one for himself and one for his partner in crime, Golden Tate. After shamelessly proclaiming themselves the best receiving duo in the nation, they grabbed yet another mic for a freshman girl they spotted in the front row. Katie wore a blue t-shirt with the words "Muck Fichigan" printed across it in bright maize yellow. Mike asked her what her shirt said, so she timidly repeated the words into her microphone. The students went ballistic. Then Golden asked her what her shirt *really* said. She seemed hesitant to cuss in front of about a thousand of her classmates, but the peer pressure was too tough to overcome. After all, it was peer pressure coming from the best receiving duo in the nation. She read the words again, this time switching the "M" and the "F" around. I honestly thought Stepan would crash down around us from the students' response.

Grabbing all three mics, I handed one to Charlie Weis while speaking into the other two. Amidst the howling feedback, my voice boomed, "What better opportunity to introduce the only adult lucky enough to get an invite tonight? I want you all to look around right now at what we have here. *This* is the spirit of Notre Dame. And this speaker once stood as one of you at rallies just like this, embracing the same spirit we're reviving here tonight. Give it up for a man who left four Super Bowl rings behind to come and coach his Alma Mater...Charlie Weis!"

Coach Weis looked like a kid in a candy store as a smirk spread across his face. He went with a straightforward approach, saying we would simply destroy Michigan. Then he told us how events like these reminded him of the fun he had as a Notre Dame student. His final words of wisdom: "Just remember...We are Notre Dame, and *they're not*!"

I saved the best for last, waiting until the racket died down a bit to introduce our emotional leader, Sergio Brown: "Our next speaker is a force to be reckoned with. He puts the *dread* in dreadlock...and he's gonna make Michigan's new "X Factor," Denard Robinson, wish he knew how to tie his shoes when he knocks them straight off his feet in front of 100,000-plus in the Big House. I promise you no one will show off a prettier back flip or a bigger smile than this guy after we win on Saturday. You know who I'm talkin' 'bout...our fearless senior defensive back, Sergiooo *Brown*!"

Sergio took my dreadlock reference to the next level by shaking his hair to the rhythm of the band as they played an intro song for him. His speech was short, but oh so sweet: "Notre Dame, listen! I'm going to Michigan to do two things: chew bubble gum, and kick ass! And guess what! I'm all outta bubblegum..." He spit a big pink wad onto the stage. It was the perfect ending to a perfect evening. The team performed their sped-up version of our fight song, and then the band joined in for a second go-around. I remembered my promise to the Dawgs, so I prayed a quick Hail Mary before taking a backwards leap of faith off the stage into their outstretched arms. I could see why rock stars loved that so much. Crowd surfing instantly became my new favorite sport.

Regis and Kelly discussed the Notre Dame versus Michigan matchup the next morning. Kelly said she thought we would win because we had a new Leprechaun. Regis explained that we get a new Leprechaun every season, but she insisted that an especially lucky one represented the Fighting Irish this year. I was pretty sure she had a major crush on me.

My friends teased me about my status as a celebrity's fake-beau when we boarded the bus to Ann Arbor around 8:30 a.m. After a swift three-hour drive we pulled up to a sprawling campus dotted with horrid pee-yellow t-shirts. I asked our bus driver if he hit a skunk along the way, but then I realized I was standing in the middle of a rancid Skunkbear nest. A multitude of middle fingers pointed our way as our police escort brought us up to the Big House. They only pumped us up even more. The spirit leftover from our sendoff rally juxtaposed against so much hatred concentrated in one place would surely help our boys in blue and gold flatten the Skunkbears like road kill.

The only kind faces we came across belonged to the Ann Arbor Police, who became our personal chauffeurs for the day. They drove us in golf carts all the way from the Big House to the tailgate boldly hosted by the Notre Dame Club of Ann Arbor behind enemy lines on the University of Michigan Golf Course. Speeding past packs of Skunkbears like that created an interesting dynamic. They all felt the need to heckle me as I zoomed by, but they only had enough time to yell out a few choice words. Most of those words only contained four letters. Since I happened to be moving far too fast for any of them to get their hands on me, I decided to have some fun with them in return. Every time someone yelled "Go Blue!" in my face, I quickly added "...and Gold!" The usual response I got consisted of nothing more than a blank stare. To every "Where's your pot of gold?" or "Where'd you hide your lucky charms?" I responded with, "They're safe back home in South Bend. Where'd you leave your dignity?" The puzzled looks continued. Whenever anyone did anything especially obscene, I just blew kisses back at them. That did the trick by making them all the more irate. I continued blowing kisses until kickoff.

When I walked into the Big House, I immediately recognized one thing we lacked at Notre Dame: color cohesiveness. Not only did over 100,000 maize t-shirts sting my retinas, but they also added to the overall intimidation factor generated by such a huge stadium. Nothing could match the euphoric feeling of running out onto the field as 81,000 fans sent a volley cheer on high over Notre Dame

Stadium. Still, the earth-shattering sound of over 100,000 fans booing the instant I appeared on their turf gave me a different kind of rush. I actually enjoyed being the focus of so much hatred all at once. Their negative energy provoked me into adopting a realistically pugnacious Fightin' Irish attitude. After all, I didn't come to Ann Arbor for a vacation. Far from it.

The game turned into a shootout as both offenses moved the ball at will. I continued to taunt the crowd throughout the first half, even after we gave up a 94-yard kickoff return for a touchdown. I loved mimicking the referees with over-exaggerated motions every time the Skunkbears committed a penalty, and I made sure to let everyone within earshot know whenever we gained a first down. At one point we converted on a third-and-long situation, so I turned to the Skunkbears in the front row: "Hey, you! Did you just see that? No? Really, though. I wasn't watching. Could you tell me what just happened? I'm confused. I know it was just third down, so how could it possibly be first down now? Did I miss something?" They sure loved showing off their middle fingers out there in the Big House.

The Skunkbears marched right down our throats during their first possession of the second half, only to miss a field goal when I waved it wide right. I took full credit. Despite their miscues, we squandered chance after chance with costly penalties and turnovers. Then, just as the fourth quarter began with the Skunkbears facing a fourth-and-three situation, Tate Forcier split our defense in half with a

31-yard touchdown run. He flipped the ball directly at me with a cocky chuckle, and it took every ounce of strength I had left in me to hold back my shillelagh. I wondered what sort of penalty the referee would have given me.

We found ourselves down by two scores late in the game, but the Fighting Irish refused to quit. A touchdown from Clausen to Tate, something I suspected I might see a few more times in the coming weeks, preceded an interception by Kyle McCarthy, another welcome sight I guessed I might get to experience again in the near future. Then Armando Allen scored on a perfectly executed Statue of Liberty play, our defense forced a punt, and we suddenly had the ball back with a three-point lead and only five minutes to go. Questionable play calling gave the Skunkbears one final shot with two minutes remaining, but I thought we had the game won when my Dawg John Ryan sacked Forcier as the clock fell below the minute mark.

With each painful, dagger-twisting completion, Forcier brought the Skunkbears that much closer to me while I watched helplessly from the corner of the end zone. There was nothing I could do, and it killed me. He capped off his brilliantly executed two-minute drill with a touchdown right in my face as time expired. I had a view that most sports fans would rather die than have to endure. Hearing that vomit-inducing "Hail to the Victors" song for what seemed like the millionth time only made our gut-wrenching 38-34 loss that much worse. Everyone watching on ESPN around the world saw the camera zoom in on me standing hunched over, sick to my stomach.

Week Three

Notre Dame Fighting Irish
vs.
Michigan State Spartans

Battle for the Megaphone Trophy

Notre Dame Stadium
Notre Dame, IN

"Nothing will ease my pain until we ruthlessly beat Sparty into submission next Saturday." I couldn't remember who I said that to, or what publication it appeared in, but a long talk with my supervisors about political correctness left those words fresh in my mind when Declan O'Kelly called for another IrishCentral.com interview. I did my best to echo the same sentiment, but in a much more appropriate manner. Declan's leading headline read, "Notre Dame Leprechaun in Fighting Irish form for crunch clash against Michigan State." His article captured the sense of urgency going into what I called a "make-or-break game." I told him I expected a fight, but the time had come for our team to make a statement. We had a long proud history of beating the odds, and we weren't about to hang our heads after just one loss.

My confidence level peaked just in time for the Friday night pep rally. Performing as the Gold Leprechaun had become second nature by that point, and I no longer felt the need to switch in and out of character. I *was* the Leprechaun. People recognized me as such whether or not I wore the green suit, so I wanted to live up to my temporary celebrity status by representing Notre Dame to the best of my ability. Every night when I got down on my knees to pray, I asked for the capacity to appreciate every moment. My one Golden year wouldn't last forever, and I intended to squeeze every last drop of glory out of it while I still could.

All that praying made me realize that my position as the Gold Leprechaun actually served as a pretty good metaphor for my life. I wanted to enjoy it, uphold a sense of honor and self-respect, live in the moment, share my joy with loved ones, and inspire as many people as possible during the short window I had. My success as the Leprechaun, and in life, would depend on my ability to use the position God put me in as best I could. Revitalized by my new outlook, I felt ready to put my soul into leaving a lasting impression on everyone I met in the name of Notre Dame. If one of those people just so happened to be Sparty, then I would have to consider leaving a different type of lasting impression on him.

As an added bonus to the already evident hype surrounding our game, the rally would serve as a 60th-reunion celebration for the 1949 Fighting Irish football team. The Lads of '49 contributed 10 impressive wins to a 38-game streak that included 36 wins, two ties, zero losses, three national championships, and two Heisman trophies over the course of four years. All that despite several star players along with head coach Frank Leahy leaving to proudly serve our country in the armed forces during World War II. These guys were real American heroes, and their story solidified Notre Dame as America's favorite college team. I didn't feel worthy when they joined me onstage, yet each one of them told me they felt honored to join *my* pep rally. The pressure was on.

Our new venue at the Irish Green made me skeptical at first, mainly due to the cotton-candy stands and bounce houses surrounding the stage. I thought I was about to host a football rally, not perform as Mickey Mouse. Luckily, my worries evaporated as more and more fans joined the small gathering of students surrounding the stage until a sea of people extended as far as the eye could see. Most important, a sizeable pack of Dawgs dressed in "bro" apparel marched right up to the stage to hear their blessed brother John Ryan speak. They waved the "Delta Omega Gamma" flag proudly while the band played our fight song and our team took the stage along with their much smaller counterparts from 1949.

The promotions staff signaled for me to start right away, so I got on with my introductions: "It's a true honor to share the stage with our 1949 national champions here tonight..." I had to pause for a well-deserved standing ovation. Leahy's Lads soaked it all in with smiles that could only come from lives well lived. "...and it's fitting that we asked our first speaker to come up and say a few words tonight. He personifies the word honor. He lives his life like a true Fightin' Irishman. He flies around that field on defense and special teams, and he is without a doubt the hardest working football player I have ever seen. Hell, he even comes from the blue collar workin' town of Cleveland, Ohio! And, as anyone who has ever been to a Dawg Hockey game already knows, he was blessed with the true Irish gift of gab. He's a trash talker with a heart of gold and a work ethic our '49 team would be proud of. It's *my* honor to introduce Alumni Hall's favorite son, high flyin' Johnyyy *Ryan*!" My Dawgs and I had been through a lot together. I had seen them get wild on several occasions, but nothing compared to the pride-filled frenzy they unleashed after that introduction.

John started out with a much-appreciated shout-out: "Let's hear it for Leprechaun Dan. He does a great job." My Dawgs awarded me with the second standing ovation of the night. Once they quieted down, John's speech left thousands in awe. He spoke about the importance of bouncing back from difficult times without losing faith. Then he saluted everyone who believed as much as he did that his team would rise up to overcome. It was almost too good to cheer for. The crowd stood in quiet reverence until he blurted out "*Alumni*!" and his Dawgs broke the silence.

With the mic back in my hand, I launched into story time: "Last year I played power forward for our All-Leprechaun team during the bookstore basketball tournament. Considering our average height, we knew we probably wouldn't rely too much on our down-low presence. Little did we know our next speaker would walk out onto the court to join our opponents. He made it pretty clear we were in trouble. At one point we grappled for the ball and he lifted me into the air over his 6'8" frame while I held on for dear life. True story. He dominated us on the court just like he's gonna dominate on the field tomorrow. Give it up for the first offensive lineman in the history of Notre Dame Football to start every game as a freshman, sophomore, junior, and now as a senior…*Sam Young*!"

Sam said he felt humbled by the '49 team, who had somehow found perfection with a 10-0 record. He wanted to compare the current Fighting Irish to another national championship team, though. After losing their second game, the '77 team went on to take the rest of their opponents by storm. They never looked back after winning their third game, and they credited that early loss as the turning point of their national–championship run. Sam didn't want to make any guarantees, but he did promise that every single guy standing behind him would come out to play every game with the heart of a champion. The crowd ate it up. It was getting real emotional out there.

I lightened the mood a bit with my next introduction: "Not only does our next speaker like to steal my style after every game when he snatches my green hat off my head for the Alma Mater, but he also stole my style by playing football exactly the same way I played in high school. Seriously, the little dude uses his size—or lack thereof—to his advantage by running over, under, around, and through his opponents. I even heard he installed mirrors on the bottom of his cleats this week so Sparty can see his own sad reflection as he runs past him on his way to the end zone! Let me introduce the only man with enough style to pull that off...Armandooo *Allen*!"

Armando immediately grabbed my hat, placing it on his own head as he began his speech. Unfortunately, I missed most of the jokes he used to slay the crowd. The promotions staff pulled me aside to inform me that I had one final guest speaker to introduce. Someone passed me the torn-off corner of a sheet of paper that simply read: "Walt Grothaus, C, 1949." I went with it.

"Sixty years ago this next man played on a team for which losing was not an option. They fought and won in every game, and in the middle of it all stood their fearless center, Walt Grothaus." My improvisation did well enough to generate yet another standing ovation for Walt, who proceeded to sing every single word to "Hike, Notre Dame!" while the band played along. Impressed that he remembered words that had long been forgotten by the student body, everyone in front of the stage honored him with a slow clap. Addressing his old teammates, he spoke about the way they simply knew how to win back in 1949. Turning to the current team, he told them he knew they would remember how to win starting tomorrow. I thought I heard a collective "I hope so" come from the crowd.

After Walt's speech I concluded the rally by sharing one final thought with the crowd: "Tomorrow let's make sure Michigan State knows this is *not* Sparta.... This is *Notre*

Dame...and we are...ND!" Everyone responded with a "WE ARE ND!" chant except for my Dawgs, who chanted "Stage dive! Stage dive!" I happily obliged. Several fans approached me afterwards to say they had never been to a more spirited rally. That meant a lot to me. I loved being able to create something special that fans could come away from feeling excited to be alive.

Every Leprechaun knew that Sparty had always been our only natural enemy. The extra significance of our mascot rivalry made showing him up on local television that much better. When WNDU-TV invited us to co-anchor their pre-game sports segment early Saturday morning, they must have forgotten that Sparty couldn't speak. I ended up running the show all by myself, while Sparty literally disappeared in front of the green screen as he attempted in vain to act out the weather like some deranged version of charades. The best part of my newscasting debut came backstage when I discovered that four separate Michigan State students actually shared their role as Sparty. Apparently, none of them could handle the rigors of a full game day on their own. I couldn't wait to laugh about it later on with my fellow Leprechauns.

Metallica woke me up from my post-news nap, but I decided to get in the zone with Warren G and Nate Dogg's "Regulate" on repeat. I donned the lucky navy blue tie with little green shamrocks and Celtic knots that I bought in Dublin two summers before. I really wanted to save it for a bowl game, but desperate times called for desperate measures. There was no way I could live with a 1-2 record. Fully dressed and looking fresh to death, I set off with the rest of the cheerleaders on our campus-wide game day publicity tour.

We got a pleasant surprise when we came across Ara Parseghian and Tom Pagna signing autographs in the bookstore. The famous duo coached together for 11 years, winning 95 games and two national championships during that span. Luckily Charles knew how to work my digital camera. I just *had* to get a picture with two of my favorite Notre Dame legends.

Somewhere between all the photo opps in front of various tailgates across campus, a middle-aged man approached me while carrying a faded green ball cap with a worn-out interlocking "ND" stitched onto the front. He told me that his father had just passed away three days earlier, and he had come to watch the game from the seats they had planned to sit in together. His father was a lifelong fan of the Fighting Irish, and there was nowhere else on earth he would rather be than Notre Dame Stadium. The man apologized for getting choked up when he offered me two hundred bucks to place his father's favorite hat on the 50-yard line after we won the game. I found myself less capable of holding back tears when I told him not to worry about the money. His hat would find its way to midfield after the win. He thanked me over and over, and then turned to go. There I stood, frozen in my tracks and crying in the middle of campus with thousands of happy football fans all around me. I didn't know what to do or say, so I yelled "Go Irish!" after him as he walked away. He turned, smiled, gave me two thumbs up, and was gone.

Still visibly shaken from what I had just witnessed, I tucked the old ball cap away in my backpack while I ran to catch up with the cheerleaders. Wow. The true meaning of Notre Dame had just stared me right in the face, turning the simple act of placing a hat on top of some grass into something so much more. Charles had forgotten all about Leprechaun duty when I fell behind, but I let it slide this time.

I barely made it back into position for the Step-Off Parade. Ushers cleared the sidewalks to make way for the band, but one elderly gentleman broke through the line to shake my hand. He told me he became my biggest fan when he saw me work the crowd at the pep rally two weeks earlier. Without warning, the gentleman then proceeded to unbutton his dress shirt to reveal the t-shirt he wore underneath. Printed on the t-shirt was a photo of me posing…with him! Mind blown, I told him I *had* to get a picture with him wearing that shirt so I could make it into a shirt of my own. He went on laughing hysterically until the ushers dragged him off to the edge of the sidewalk.

I reserved some of my energy during the Step-Off Parade just in case I happened to find myself in an altercation with my nemesis Sparty at some point during the game.

He surprisingly kept his distance throughout the entire pre-game warm-up, so I decided to be a good little Leprechaun and let him go. Public shaming on the local news was good enough for me. Their cheerleading squad did come over to our sideline for a cheer challenge, though. The contest consisted of a guy from each squad holding a girl up in the air for as long as possible with just one hand. We didn't technically cheat, but we did match Big Dave up with Tiny Courtney. We won by a landslide, and Dave even cranked out a few shoulder presses with Courtney as his dumbbell to the delight of our student section. Vince Vaughn stopped by to congratulate them on their victory. Only at Notre Dame.

The game got off to a flying start, with Jimmy Clausen completing a perfect 10 out of 10 passes in the first quarter. Then the luck of the Irish began to fade a bit during the second quarter when Jimmy went down with a foot injury and Michael Floyd got knocked out of the game on a touchdown catch ruled incomplete by incompetent officials. I made one of the refs pay for his habitual bad calls, albeit accidently, when I ran headlong into him while sprinting along the sideline during a big play. After we both got up and dusted ourselves off, he scolded me pretty mercilessly, even threatening to throw a flag on me if it ever happened again. I made sure to keep my distance from then on.

Armando Allen and Golden Tate stepped up in Jimmy's absence, running the "Wild Leprechaun" option-read offense to a tee. Still, several missed tackles later we found ourselves down 30-26 midway through the fourth quarter. Then Jimmy hobbled back into the game to give us the lead with a perfect toss to his favorite target in the corner of the end zone. Golden must have thought our band would catch him when he celebrated the go-ahead score with a swan dive. Instead, he ended up crushing the scrawny kid holding a French horn in the middle of the Michigan State band while Sparty stood by motionless. I prayed that play would end up as the winning touchdown so ESPN could feature it on their Top-10 as well as their Not-Top-10.

Flashbacks of Tate Forcier haunted me as Kirk Cousins slowly but steadily moved Michigan State into field-goal range with the clock ticking down. I waited with painstaking agony for something, anything, to happen. Then, out of nowhere, Kyle McCarthy swooped in to save the day with an interception at the four-yard line. My sigh of relief felt much better than the excruciating groan I let out when our last game ended. Nail-biters were way more fun from the winning side.

Jimmy limped back out onto the field to ice the clock, and Heisman talk continued after his 300-yard, two-touchdown performance. I gladly gave Armando my hat in honor of his career day, which included well over 100 all-purpose yards, a rushing touchdown, and even a touchdown throw. After a particularly cheerful Alma Mater, I waited for the stadium to empty. My job wasn't over until I placed that old ball cap on the 50-yard line. I jogged back through the tunnel knowing that I had just made someone out there pretty happy.

Week Four

Notre Dame Fighting Irish vs. Purdue Boilermakers

Battle for the Shillelagh Trophy

Ross-Ade Stadium
West Lafayette, IN

After two straight barnburners against Michigan and Michigan State, we all looked forward to taking a drive through farm country down to West Lafayette for a bit of a break against lowly Purdue. I honestly expected a smash-up job—in and out. Wham, bam, thank you, Boilermakers. Unfortunately, plenty of tractors along US-31 turned our two-hour road trip into a four-hour traffic jam. We pulled up to Ross-Ade Stadium just minutes before kickoff.

Our travel difficulties actually provided a nice change of pace. With no pre-game appearances to worry about, we could focus all our attention on the game. I wanted to do everything I could to help our team get out of there with a win. If that involved demoralizing their fans by obnoxiously showboating all game long, then so be it. "Purdon't" became the word of the day, and I repeated it frequently to pretty much every Purdue fan within ear-shot. I didn't expect it to instigate such an angry backlash, nor did I expect their fans to turn into such discourteous hosts. To be honest, I wasn't even convinced that Purdue football fans actually existed until I saw 59,000 of them wearing black t-shirts as part of their unsuccessful attempt to intimidate us with a stadium-wide "black out."

We waited outside the designated away-team tunnel as the Boilermakers prepared to take the field. I looked forward to seeing what sorts of bells and whistles they would use to accent their dramatic arrival, but I mostly just wanted to hear the Bronx cheer they would welcome me with when I sprinted out onto their field waving the Blue and Gold. Describing what I saw next as bells and whistles wouldn't have done it any justice. Their team ran out through an imitation railroad tunnel complete with fake train tracks and a blinking sign that read, "Boiler Crossing." I laughed out loud when members of their color guard scampered about in shiny silver helmets beating a relatively small drum with the words "World's Largest" painted on the side. Where the hell was I? When their entire student section let out a loud "Toot! Toot!" I came to accept the fact that they took their trains rather seriously down there in the heartland.

I could have heard a pin drop when I led our team out onto the field. Ross-Ade Stadium was no Big House. Their fans must have felt the need to compensate, because what they lacked in noise they sure made up for with downright disrespectful behavior. Our poor sweet cheerleaders stood by in total disbelief as disgruntled fans spit all over their backpacks, which they apparently placed much too close to the front row. These were grown men sitting with their children right beside them. The language spewing forth from their uncouth mouths was impolite at best. I combated their coarseness in true Notre Dame fashion. I killed them with kindness. Smiles, waves, and kisses blown in their general direction worked wonders. Whenever they said anything particularly nasty, I ran up to give their kids high-fives. Handing each of their sons and daughters little blue ribbons with "Go Irish! Beat Purdue!" printed in gold, I did my best to convert them before it was too late. By the time both teams lined up for the opening kick, most of their kids had already begun chanting, "Let's go, Irish!" along with our cheerleaders.

My over-exaggerated etiquette gave way to frustration when we found ourselves losing 7-3 after a first quarter filled with missed tackles. The banter flying back and forth between me and the fans in the front row took a turn for the worse: "Hey, Leprechaun! Nice Capri pants! You must be the biggest loser at Notre Dame!"

"Hey, farmer John! I'll take the biggest loser at Notre Dame over the coolest guy at Purdue any day!"

"Oh, yeah? Did you fly here on a freakin' rainbow?"

"No, we chartered a bus. Actually, I think I remember you! Didn't we pass your tractor along the way? What's the top speed on that thing? Fifteen?"

We must have caused quite the commotion, because in almost no time the ill-constructed papier-mâché mascot named Purdue Pete came over to get in the mix. He clearly wanted to milk his team's four-point lead as much as he could while it still lasted, so he danced around like a lout behind my back. I didn't really mind, but for some reason the fans in the front row decided it was the funniest thing they had ever seen. I couldn't allow them to have any more fun at my expense, so I enlisted the Irish Guard to go on "Purdue Pete duty." The next time he got too close, they forcibly removed him. After all, Indiana state law still applied in West Lafayette.

Clearly not himself, Jimmy Clausen struggled early on as he battled with his foot injury. Fortunately, our highly touted sophomore quarterback Dayne Crist came in to finish out the first half with two gutsy touchdown drives. His heroics allowed us to jog off the field with a 17-7 lead. The cheerleaders and I made our way up the away-team tunnel, but the Purdue promotions staff pointed us in the opposite direction. Apparently their cheerleaders wanted to host us for a nice little snack break. Their food tasted much better than it would have *before* Dayne's last two touchdowns.

I should have known it was a trap. Halfway through my locally grown farm-fresh apple, I nearly choked when Purdue Pete came storming in with his sledgehammer pointed straight at me. I realized how real it was when it connected with the wall just inches from my head. With both of us ready to throw down, his cheerleaders pulled him away while apologizing. Not taking my cue to cut off all association with this madman, I mouthed off: "Why so angry? It's not like this is a rivalry game or anything. You go to Purdue. You don't belong on a football field, and you will *never* be our rival."

I may have taken it a little too far. Petey-boy broke free from the tiny girls holding him back, getting as close as possible to my face before making several strong statements laced with even stronger language. The whole room fell silent, and his cheerleaders mouthed, "I'm so sorry!" as they slowly pulled him out of sight. Realizing that I probably shouldn't fraternize with our enemies any more, I decided to swear off snack time cold turkey.

Touchdowns were tough to come by in the second half, though I did score some extra style points when I embarrassed little Petey during the split screen dance-off they featured on their video board. I wished I could have seen the look of humiliation on his face, but it was covered in cardboard. A few minutes later, I found myself much more thankful for his homemade mask. He couldn't even smile when his team scored twice in a row to take a 21-17 lead.

After Golden Tate somehow kept us in the game by running our offense as an option-read quarterback, Jimmy literally hopped out to the huddle on one foot with under four minutes to go. Eighty-eight yards later, he connected with Golden on a 17-yard rocket to set us up with a first-and-goal situation at the four-yard line. Then first down turned into fourth down with only 25 seconds left, and I felt like I was about to suffer my third heart attack in three weeks. It all came down to one last play. In the blink of an eye, one of our players dove to the turf, holding the ball extended into the air as he lay in the end zone. I couldn't see who it was because a mosh pit of players surrounded him, but I should have guessed that Kyle Rudolph would come through in the clutch. The ref had to pull me off the field after I got in the pit with everyone except Jimmy, who gave a fist pump from afar as he slowly made his way back to the sideline in obvious pain.

Golden deserved to wear my Leprechaun hat after gaining over 50 yards on the ground and 50 more through the air as a running back, wide receiver, and option quarterback. He showed off his fancy footwork with a jig directed at the Fighting Irish fans who made their way down towards the away-team tunnel to celebrate our 24-21 victory. The Purdue fans surrounding us didn't look too happy, but we all wore gigantic grins as we swayed to our Alma Mater. I was so happy to escape with a win that I almost didn't hear a voice call out, "Hey, Leprechaun! I'm an Irish girl! Can I get a picture?" I gave Erin Andrews my phone number so she could send me the photo we took together, but for some reason she never got back to me.

Week Five
Notre Dame Fighting Irish
vs.
Washington Huskies

Notre Dame Stadium
Notre Dame, IN

By my third home game as the Gold Leprechaun, I picked up a pretty regular routine, fraught with superstition, of course. If the Fighting Irish won, I had to do everything in the exact same sequence leading up to the next game. When my classes finished for the week on Thursday afternoon, I joined the promotions staff for an on-site pep rally walk-through. Then came my weekly morale-boosting visit to Club Fever for "College Night," highlighted by skipping long lines and dancing onstage with the cheerleaders. After shutting down "The Feve" around 3 a.m., I crashed back in Alumni Hall until noon on Friday when I walked to South Dining Hall for something deliciously greasy to soak up my hangover. Once I got back to my room, I checked my email to find out the person(s) I would introduce at the pep rally later that evening. Then I came up with my introduction(s), while carefully crafting my chinstrap beard, stopping only to supplement my speeches with extra research. At some point, every Leprechaun came to develop his own specific style of facial hair.

I liked to keep mine thick enough to seem caricature-like, yet groomed well enough to look sharp.

If representing Notre Dame as the Gold Leprechaun was the best job on campus, then working as an admissions tour guide came in a close second place. Every Friday afternoon I got paid to walk around campus backwards while talking to prospective students and their families. My boss gave me a script to memorize, but I told Leprechaun war stories instead. I usually tried to gear up in as much free Adidas swag as possible and, on cold days, I even wore my varsity jacket with "Leprechaun" stitched across the big gold shamrock on its left breast. High school students, their siblings, and especially their moms ate it up. We took photos together in front of the Golden Dome, Touchdown Jesus, and Notre Dame Stadium. Then I told them to come find me after the pep rally that night to complete their photo sets by getting some shots with me in my Leprechaun suit. Some of the best and brightest students coming out of any high school in the nation chose Notre Dame because of my tours. I had the tip money from their parents to prove it.

As soon as I dropped my new friends off back at the Golden Dome, I stopped by Saint Michael's Laundry on the north edge of campus to pick up my dry cleaning.
Lots of double takes and quick snapshots came my way while I walked back to Alumni Hall carrying my freshly cleaned, vivid green Leprechaun suit on a hanger. Back in my room, I enjoyed my perfect view of the band marching across South Quad to their pre-rally practice. Every time

they launched into our fight song, a feeling came over me that I wished I could put into words. I tried to capture that sentiment as I practiced my introduction speeches one final time while suiting up. First came my white button-down shirt and knee-high socks, then my green knickers and whatever tie looked particularly lucky that day, followed by my gold vest, green jacket, unscuffed Adidas, and the bowler hat I had shaped by hand to look like it belonged to an Irish cowboy.

Without fail, my Dawgs in the room next door would commence their "40s at 4" celebration right around the same time I finished getting dressed. I loved stopping by their parties just as they got into full swing so I could surprise the weekly mix of students, parents, and alums as they enjoyed the finest malt liquor money could buy. The looks on their faces were priceless, and they often thanked me for getting their weekend off to a lucky start. Though I politely refused to partake in the toasts they raised to the Fighting Irish, I always made sure to pose for a rare photo opp before heading off to the rally. With a tracksuit covering my Leprechaun getup, I usually made it to the Irish Green on time. Only one or two of the most watchful fans tended to stop me after spotting my green coattails hanging out of my blue and gold Adidas jacket. Once I made it to the venue, I waited backstage while getting ready to do my thing on the mic.

Before this particular rally I had an appointment with "The Catholic Guy" for a live talk-show interview on

Sirius Radio. I had no idea what to expect, so I brought my trusty bodyguard Charles with me just in case things got out of hand. We took the elevator up to the press box in Notre Dame Stadium, where we saw none other than our University president, Father John Jenkins, waiting to join the show for an interview of his own. At that point I felt more than intimidated, thinking a quiz on the basic tenets of Catholicism was soon to follow. Far from it. The Catholic Guy actually ended up giving both Charles and me headsets and sitting us down ahead of Father Jenkins for an informal chat about the spirit of Notre Dame. He asked us all the familiar questions we had grown accustomed to answering about tryouts and traveling with the football team. Then he asked if joining the cheerleading squad helped with the ladies, and Charles jumped in to make it clear that we got to hang out with the prettiest girls on campus every day at practice. The Catholic Guy told us we had it all figured out. His final words of wisdom: "Keep livin' the dream, boys." After the interview, I apologized to Father Jenkins for making him wait. He graciously told me not to worry about it, thanking me for going first to set the tone.

Charles and I made our way out of Notre Dame Stadium after a few photo opps in the press box, and then we jogged towards the sound of the band. The temperature had fallen noticeably during our interview, and big cold raindrops slapped me in the face as I ran. Undeterred by the typical South Bend weather, thousands of fans flooded the southern edge of campus for our rally. We caught up with the band, marched right into the Irish Green, and rocked that crowd.

"Notre Daaame! Before we get started I need to share somethin' that a good friend of mine recently brought to my attention.... You see, apparently the coaches and players out in Washington decided to do a little bit of trash talkin' this week.... They didn't say anything at all about our football team, though. Nope. They decided to talk trash about all of *you*! They decided to talk trash about our students, they decided to talk trash about our fans, and they decided to talk trash about our stadium! You believe that?" By the sound of their booming response, I could tell my fellow Fighting Irish fans felt just as outraged as I did.

"Now, get this. A local Washington newspaper even quoted their coaching staff talkin' 'bout how *quiet* it gets inside Notre Dame Stadium. Yet they still felt the need to blast our fight song on repeat during their practices all week long. And what did they say about the greatest of all university fight songs? They said it gets 'kind of mind numbing' after two hours. Whoa...Wait a minute...Two hours? They must not know what they're talkin' about because they're not gonna stop hearin' our fight song after just *two hours* tomorrow... Not a chance... They'll be hearin' our fight song *in their sleep* tomorrow night after the Band of the Fightin' Irish blasts it every time we score touchdown, after touchdown, *after touchdown*! You feel me?" Another uproar. They felt me.

"Now, without further ado...please join me in welcoming the men who plan on makin' sure we hear our fight song on repeat all game long.... Give it up for *your* 2009 University of Notre Dame Fightin' Irish!" Clearly pumped up by the props I just gave them, our band blared every note of our fight song over and over while the football players slowly made their way onto the stage.

"We're about to get our first speaker on the mic in just a few seconds. I bet you've heard his name before, but you probably don't know his story. That's a shame, because his story *is* Notre Dame. He's a walk-on player who *earned* his scholarship through nothing but toughness, pure perseverance, and a fightin' spirit that never quits. Every time he steps onto the football field he plays with unmatched intensity, and that's because he's livin' the dream out there in Notre Dame Stadium. He's a little dude who makes big plays on special teams.... Let's hear it for Mike *Anello*!"

Walk-on players always held a special place within our football program. They epitomized the spirit of Notre Dame. The Fighting Irish attitude shared by guys who truly fought to earn their keep, like Mike Anello, Bobby Burger, Nick Lezynski, the Coughlin brothers, and the Salvis, kept that never-say-die, hard-knock spirit alive year after year. I always imagined that if Rockne could come back to meet our current team he would start by shaking the hands of every single walk-on player. They were a band of brothers, and Mike's speech represented them well. Most of the crowd added their teardrops to the rain-soaked grass when he told them that he really did get to "live the dream" every day he spent at Notre Dame. He thanked his family for the sacrifices that made his dream possible, and he saluted his new Notre Dame Family for giving him the chance to share his dream with so many. His journey was about more than just football. It was about life. When he finished speaking, the crowd applauded him with reverence, undoubtedly reflecting on the example he set for their own lives.

When I saw what our next speaker was holding behind his back, I decided to have some fun with his introduction: "When Kerry Neal crosses the street, cars stop to look both ways. Actually, they named a street on campus after Kerry Neal. They had to change it, though. No one crosses Kerry Neal and lives to tell about it. That's probably why Washington's running backs haven't slept a wink all week. They're scared of having nightmares about Kerry Neal. Don't feel bad for them, though. They'll finally get some sleep tomorrow afternoon when he knocks them into next week." Kerry didn't even need to say anything. He simply pulled the stuffed toy husky out from behind his back, tore its head off, and punted it into the crowd. Synthetic fur and fuzzy foam stuffing flew all over. Our band played Darth Vader's theme song and we all chanted, "Kill! Kill! Kill!" to the beat.

Things were getting pretty heated. I expected everyone to calm down a bit when our next speaker took the stage, but I was wrong. Ned Bolcar didn't even let me finish my introduction before he began scolding the crowd for their lack of enthusiasm. I thought they seemed pretty excited, but according to Ned they looked far too lackadaisical for a pep rally. He paced back and forth, screaming into his mic until every last man, woman, and child cheered to reassure him that they were in fact awake. I formally introduced him when he stopped to apologize for the four-letter words he had just let slip.

"I'm not sure he needs much more of an introduction than that, but let's give him a warm welcome. He proudly served as a co-captain on the 1988 national championship Fightin' Irish football team. He played a major part in twenty-three straight victories under legendary coach Lou Holtz, the longest winning streak since the days of Frank Leahy's lads during World War II. He gave his team that extra element you might expect from a New Jersey guy who needs an extra neck pad just to keep himself from getting hurt by his own bone-crushing hits. Please welcome one of the greatest of all time, *Ned Bolcar*!"

Ned continued his spirited speech, looking directly at the current players as he spoke about what it means to become a Notre Dame Man. He told them to act with the sense of self-respect expected of them, while also coming at their opponents with the fury of true Fighting Irishmen. Turning to the fans, he warned that he better not catch any of them sleeping inside Notre Dame Stadium the next day. He promised to bring his extra neck pad along just in case. As I surveyed the crowd, I noticed laughter mixed with looks of genuine fear while everyone linked arms for the Alma Mater.

Buckets of ice water dumped on us the next day when we attempted to make our usual pre-game rounds. Most of our regular tailgate rallies fell victim to extensive rain delays. The familiar enthusiastic game-day feel seemed to wash away along with the rivers of water pouring down every storm drain on campus, so the cheerleaders and I took shelter in the Joyce Center. We waited out the storm while making several return trips to the Monogram Club for more food. With no other way to let out all that pep we had stored up for game day, we resorted to cheering on Mike as he made his way through pounds and pounds of pulled pork.

As so often happened at Notre Dame, one bright spot shined through our otherwise stormy day. My dad introduced me to his new friend just prior to the Step-Off Parade. Tom Menn sat patiently on his lucky bench, waiting for our band to strike up his favorite song. After watching us march by, he planned to take a shortcut across campus so he could catch us one last time just as we entered Notre Dame Stadium. He had it down to a science, which made sense considering he did it 302 times before without missing a single home game. When they wrote our fight song to include the words "loyal sons" back at the turn of the century, the Shea brothers probably had guys like Tom in mind. He had seen it all, and I felt honored when he said he could tell that I really put everything I had into my role as the Leprechaun. He told me to keep it up. I told him to enjoy watching us win game 303.

Refusing to cease, the rain made everything exceedingly

slippery during the game. Standing at 5′1″ on a good day, Christy was my favorite cheerleader to hoist into the air. Fans loved taking pictures of her wearing my Leprechaun hat while standing on my shoulders. Some even joked that together we almost added up to the height of one Irish Guardsman. I learned not to try our shoulder-standing stunt in the rain because her tiny foot slipped on my sopping wet gold vest and I almost killed her in front of 81,000 witnesses.

Golden Tate showed everyone in Notre Dame Stadium that he had a better grip than either Christy or I when he hauled in two touchdowns on his way to 244 yards receiving. With every catch he came closer to establishing himself as the most elite wide receiver in the nation, refusing to let the Huskies drag him down into the mud. Other than his superhuman effort, the rest of the game flew by in one big wet blur. I only remembered stomping through the tunnel at halftime, fuming that we trailed by one point rather than leading by two after a missed field goal. Harry the Husky got left hanging as he held up his paw for a high-five when I came storming back out to watch the rest of our waterlogged game with my people. After my run-in with Purdue Pete, I had a promise to keep: No more fraternizing with the enemy.

I did remember the rising noise level when the game still hung in the balance as the final minutes fell off the clock. Our fans finally found their Fighting Irish fortitude just in time to fuel our defense during two straight goal-line stands. Then they fell silent just as quickly as they peaked.

We got the ball back trailing by 8, and 81,000 sets of lungs held their collective breath during the entirety of Jimmy Clausen's perfectly executed two-minute drill. The tension remained palpable until Robert Hughes bulldozed his way into the end zone for a game-tying two-point conversion. Overtime started with the low rumble of "Huuughes" still echoing throughout the student section.

The Huskies won the coin toss at the beginning of overtime, electing to give us the ball first. That didn't last long. Hughes wasted no time, rumbling into the end zone once again. That meant Washington's star signal caller, Jake Locker, would have to cap off his miracle game through the heavy rain right in front of our deafening student section. He jogged out to his huddle with a self-assured strut. Our students made him pay for such audacity. Their ear-ringing decibels shook the confidence right out of him, as did our defense. Facing fourth-and-long, he heaved one final prayer across the middle of the field.

Oh…No…

I cringed as the ball connected with a Washington receiver's fingertips at the four-yard line. Time stood still. Then, like a flash, our safeties Kyle McCarthy and Harrison Smith descended upon that receiver with the force of two soaring falcons swooping down on their prey. All three bodies collided simultaneously with perfect timing. It was pure poetry in motion. The ball flew from the receiver's fingertips, landing with a splash next to the helmet Kyle and Harry had dislodged from his head. They stood over him exultantly like predators admiring their kill. I got a running start for my celebratory mudslide across the swampy end zone. Saint Michael's Laundry would have a tough dry-cleaning job ahead of them, but it was worth it. I stood in front of the rejoicing student section, drenched to the bone, caked in mud, and chanting, "BEAT SC! BEAT SC!" along with 81,000 of my closest friends. Mike Anello was right. We were all living the dream.

Week Six

#25 Notre Dame Fighting Irish
vs.
#6 Southern Cal Trojans

Battle for the Jeweled Shillelagh

Notre Dame Stadium
Notre Dame, IN

Notre Dame versus Southern Cal, known as "the greatest intersectional rivalry in college football" since 1926, had looked nothing like a rivalry as of late. Not only had we lost seven straight times, but the infamous 2005 "Bush Push" game still haunted our collective nightmares. Our students rushed the field at the end of that game, thinking the #9 Fighting Irish had just upset the #1 Trojans, only to get turned away when the officials put one second back on the clock. Southern Cal's running back, Reggie Bush, used that final second to steal the game from us in bizarre fashion. When I enrolled as a freshman the following year, the upperclassmen still spoke about that harrowing day as if their wounds had never fully healed. With each mounting loss, the misery returned. Our rival's reign of terror over us wasn't fun to live through, but we all held on to the small slice of hope that one day their dynasty would come to an end.

On top of the historical significance and the bitter

resentment that fueled our rivalry, I held a personal vendetta against the Trojans. One of my best friends from high school chose to attend Southern Cal seemingly just so he could refine his disdain for the Fighting Irish. I never understood how anyone could hate such a wonderfully positive place as Notre Dame, but every time I heard from him or any of his Trojan friends I sensed jealousy. Deep down under all that hatred, students at the University of Spoiled Children must have known they would never match the timeless tradition or the sense of respect generated by the Notre Dame Family. Maybe that explained why my friend wouldn't shut up when he visited to watch his #9 Trojans take on the unranked 1-6 Fighting Irish during my sophomore year. Sadly, even he stopped mocking me when his team completely crushed the life out of us with a 38-0 massacre. I couldn't think of any worse feeling than the embarrassment that came with our supposed rivals actually starting to feel sorry for us.

With a long back-story leaving an insufferably sour taste in my mouth, I decided that my senior year would have to be the one when the Fighting Irish finally turned the tables on the Trojans. Coming off an emotional overtime win against Washington, the only team to beat Southern Cal so far that season, we knew we had a chance to pull off the upset. In fact, I felt confident we would. Once I got my hands on that Jeweled Shillelagh, I planned on taking it with me everywhere I went. I just had to make sure everyone else at Notre Dame believed as much as I did.

Building hype became my sole purpose in life during the full duration of midterm week—which I renamed "Beat SC Week." It had a better ring to it. As soon as we all started chanting "BEAT SC! BEAT SC!" after our overtime win against Washington, I decided to throw all my study materials out the window for the next few days. I told myself I would remember this week years later as a defining moment in my life, and my greatest accomplishment as the Notre Dame Leprechaun. In comparison, I would probably forget everything I needed to know for my exams by the following semester. Mark Twain once advised against letting school interfere with a good education. I intended to learn a whole lot about life by allowing one goal to consume mine for the next week. I wouldn't rest until I stoked the smoldering flames of our faith in the Fighting Irish into widespread raging fires by the time our enemy arrived on campus.

When Monday morning came I got up at 6:30 a.m., rode my bike over to the computer lab, typed out "GO IRISH! KILL SOUTHERN CAL!" in 72-point type, printed out fifty copies, and taped them all to the walls outside DeBartolo Hall—where I knew the football players usually congregated before their morning classes. I figured my efforts would start the week off right with some early hype. Unfortunately, when I returned at 8:30 a.m. for my first class, only torn shreds of paper remained taped to the walls. The building managers must have taken their jobs a little too seriously that morning. Maybe one of them had a case of the Mondays. Frustrated, but not nearly ready to quit, I used the time I spent in class that day planning better ways to build more hype.

That afternoon I hosted a meeting of the minds with my two close friends Grant Schmidt and Aaron Hernandez, who happened to be the Student Body President and the Drum Major for the Band of the Fighting Irish. We came together to build a unified front, determined to use our leadership positions to make this a week our fellow students would never forget. The grassroots strategy we devised would hopefully empower the whole student body to take over our hype-building efforts by the end of the week. Rather than a packaged promotions plan coming down from upstairs, the end result would grow organically from the bottom up into something much more genuine. That way our entire Notre Dame Family would have no choice but to believe the hype.

Grant, Aaron, and I began "Beat SC Week" by coordinating a massive communications campaign, run mostly through social media, and open letters to the student body. We would get the party started, then sit back to watch the hype spread from person to person until it covered our whole campus. Getting to work right away, we invited our fellow students to join us in conveying our collective belief through posters, signs, banners, and by any other means necessary. We only asked that they keep their anti-Trojan, pro-Irish propaganda classy. Finally, we scheduled several unofficial student-run events, including a "Southern Cal Meet-n-Greet" meant to "welcome" our opponents when they first arrived for their Friday walk-through practice. We also promised to add an extra kick to our Friday night pep rally and our midnight drum circle, courtesy of our homemade Trojan Horse and some amateur pyrotechnics.

I returned to my room with my mind racingas I fired off several phone calls and emails. Everyone loved my idea to exchange "The Shirt" with something more meaningful to match the magnitude of our rivalry. I didn't even have to launch into my long-winded narrative about the relevant connotations of the color green. My fellow diehards promised that the entire student section would sport lovely shades of Kelly, Hunter, and Emerald on Saturday. Most of the presidents from each dorm on campus were on board with our sign-making efforts as well but, for some reason, Dillon Hall's representative didn't seem to trust my sincerity when it came to hanging bed-sheet banners from windows. I showed my dedication to the cause by spray-painting "Kill So. Cal" across the Irish Tricolour flag I bought two summers before in Dublin. Students stopped under my window all day long to take photos of my artwork as it fluttered majestically over South Quad.

When one of my administrative supervisors summoned me in for a meeting, I knew it could be trouble. The lecture that began as soon as I walked through the door focused mainly on the need to follow protocol and work through the correct channels. Our grassroots movement didn't have room for protocol or correct channels, but I didn't waste my time arguing. After a few minutes of getting talked to, I drifted off into more daydreaming about the campus-wide cogs we had already set in motion. I smiled knowing they were churning the hype machine we created at that very moment. It was too late to go back now. The damage was done. I crossed my fingers behind my back as I promised to get everything approved from that point on. With a hop, skip, and a jump out of the administrative offices I set off to continue the task at hand.

As far as I was concerned, we were at war. In this battle of good versus evil, I wouldn't surrender until I did all that I could to help the good guys come out on top. That night I sent the first of several wartime propaganda letters out to my entire Notre Dame Family:

> Notre Dame,
>
> This is our moment of truth. We must wake up the echoes. We must let everyone know we believe. All of us have a role to play in our upcoming battle against the Trojans of Southern Cal.
>
> Students: Step up your efforts to create as much hype as possible. Post signs. Hang banners. Write on sidewalks. It's midterm week. What better way to procrastinate? Do all that you can to energize your classmates. Don't be afraid to let our football team know you believe. Share a friendly "Go Irish!" or better yet a "Kill Southern Cal!" with every football player you encounter.
>
> Fans: Wear green to campus this weekend.

> Get loud at the rally on Friday, and then come to the drum circle on the steps of the Golden Dome at midnight. Stand up and scream from the very first moment you enter Notre Dame Stadium until the final whistle when we rush onto the most sacred of all football fields. I'll see you on the 50-yard line. Look for the guy dressed in green with pure triumphant joy written all over his face.
>
> GO IRISH! KILL SOUTHERN CAL!
>
> Your Fightin' Irish Leprechaun

The hype snowballed beyond anyone's control as we watched in awe at what we created. Alums wrote in to *The Observer* to call out our students for not cheering loud enough; several students wrote back to call out all the alums who seemed to have forgotten how to cheer altogether; and a full-blown debate over appropriate fan behavior ensued in the "Letters to the Editor" section. That discourse only added to the constant conversation taking place in the dorms, dining halls, and classrooms all across campus. Our impending showdown came to dominate the thoughts of almost every well-educated mind at Notre Dame, much to the chagrin of the professors who attempted to maintain order during midterms.

Our heightened sense of anticipation continued to spread like wild fire as the week went on, almost taking on a physical presence that I could taste in the air as I walked to my classes every day. An article in *The Observer* quoted me issuing a "call to arms" to the student body, previewing an "up-tempo, raw, uncut" pep rally, and asking everyone to create a "green out" effect in Notre Dame Stadium for the game. I didn't really know what those words meant when I said them, but they looked good in print and they got people excited. As the week went on, my classmates amazed me with their passionate commitment to the cause. My good friends Dallas and Sean, two of the most devoted diehards I had ever met, constructed a life-size Trojan Horse out of plywood in the engineering building. Banners appeared on every dorm, many showcasing the types of puns expected of our sharp-witted students. Even the classics department chipped in by sponsoring the creation of a giant flag outside O'Shaughnessy Hall featuring a historically accurate depiction of a Trojan Horse beneath the words: "The Trojan Era has ended. Let the Golden Era begin."

Once it became evident what was going on, *The Observer* declared "Beat SC Week" a resounding success by printing a full-page public notice previewing our special pep rally, drum circle, and "green out." All our hard work was beginning to pay big dividends. I never thought coordinating a grassroots movement like that could be so exhilarating, and I definitely never expected to enjoy midterm week as much as I did. Yet, there we were in the middle of it all, beaming with pride. Good thing I bailed on studying for those exams. I was learning more about bringing people together and harnessing the power of the human spirit than I had gained during all my previous years of formal education combined.

Thursday morning felt like an ambush when the promotions staff alerted me that our pep rally would take place at the Irish Green rather than inside Notre Dame Stadium. Apparently, the tentative promise Grant and I secured the summer before was truly tentative all along. Unwilling to go quietly into the night, we agreed that our disappointment couldn't sidetrack us now after we had come so far. If we wanted students to show up at our rally, we had some serious work to do. I called our football office directly, trying to sound serious rather than laugh as I told the secretary that an angry Leprechaun had an urgent message for the head coach.

It was probably a good sign that Charlie Weis had bigger fish to fry, so I wasn't too upset when I ended up talking to another representative of the football program instead. Through the brief conversation that followed, I somehow got the team officially on board. They promised to run another full-page ad in *The Observer* in addition to sending an email straight from Charlie to the entire student body. Sure enough, he sent out an eloquently worded letter to the students of Notre Dame asking for their full support at the rally and the game. His love for his Alma Mater came through loud and clear, as did his expectation of "near perfect attendance."

Even after our coach saved the day, the close call left me feeling terrified that all our efforts would go unnoticed by the majority of our players, students, and fans.

The thought of setting up an epic war rally only to find no students in attendance became my biggest fear. Then, as if by providence, a semi-anonymous note found its way into my mailbox just in time to calm my nerves:

> Hey Mr. Leprechaun!
>
> I have no idea who you are, but I love you! What you're doing is absolutely amazing. I'm studying abroad all the way in Ireland, but I can tell just how much effort you're putting into this week. You make a damn good Leprechaun! When this is all said and done, I'm sure you'll be happy with what you put into it. I just wanted to say good job, keep it up, and thanks for keeping the spirit alive all over the world!
>
> GO IRISH!
> Kate

We peaked when the football team officially hopped on our bandwagon, but we weren't done yet. About 200 students started a slow-clap as the football team jogged from the practice field to the locker room after their last walk-through of the week on Thursday afternoon. That night found us back at work with a crew of loyal sons and daughters tagging every building, tree, bench, and sidewalk on campus with encouraging football-related messages written in chalk. We started at 11 p.m., hitting the high traffic areas in front of both dining halls, every major classroom building, and the Hesburgh Library. As a grand finale, we wrote "Kill Southern Cal Like A Champion Today" in big yellow block letters directly outside the entrance to the football facilities. Then we passed by the north gate of Notre Dame Stadium on our way home at 2 a.m. and I came up with an idea for one last legendary tag. The twelve-foot-tall letters spelling out "FALL OF TROY" in front of our tunnel looked flawless when we finally finished. We hoped the Trojans would appreciate the welcome gift we left them when their buses pulled up to that exact spot roughly ten hours later.

A searing hot dagger tore through my heart when I rode my bike past the cleaning crew scrubbing our artwork from the sidewalk outside Notre Dame Stadium on Friday morning. At least they left most of the tags we strategically planted in places where our football team could actually receive our message. We tried to take the setback in stride, hoping for the best. Little did we know our campaign would go worldwide when the *LA Times* and ESPN both mentioned our hype-building efforts. I could barely believe my eyes when SportsCenter featured video footage of the chalk scribbles I left on a sidewalk the night before. An editorial on ESPN.com even mentioned the handwritten messages that "covered the fabled South Bend campus." The article went on to quote our football captain Sam Young talking about how much the hype affected his teammates. We knew we were on the right track when he said it definitely helped them believe.

Friday morning came, and the students awoke to yet another letter in their mailboxes:

ATTENTION NOTRE DAME:
A CALL TO ARMS

To the Students of Our Lady's University,

As we near the end of midterms, we would like to wish all of you the best of luck with your exams. This letter concerns a different matter, though. The time has come to concentrate our collective focus on one goal: We must beat Southern Cal.

It is up to all of you to make this happen. Notre Dame needs you, and the vital role each and every one of you must play starts today. An unscripted, high energy, Fightin' Irish "Call to Arms Rally" will take place on the Irish Green. This momentous event will showcase a meaner, nastier, raw Fightin' Irish attitude. The football team requests that you all show up by 5:30 p.m. so they can arrive to an already packed house at 6 p.m. We will reserve an area directly in front of the stage for the students, but we expect you to burst beyond those confines. Legends of this weekend will echo for all of eternity after the Fighting Irish emerge from battle victorious. Come join the growing legend by sending our team off with a rally befitting a band of heroes.

This is the biggest game any of us will ever see inside Notre Dame Stadium as students. We all must rally for our football team and our University.

The fall of Troy starts today,

Grant Schmidt,
Notre Dame Student Body President
Aaron Hernandez,
Notre Dame Drum Major
Daniel Collins, Notre Dame Leprechaun

I ditched my normal routine Friday morning so I could make some signs for our "Southern Cal Meet-n-Greet" set to take place that afternoon. Then, just as I left my room carrying several cardboard gravestones with "RIP USC" written on them, promotions called me to the Irish Green for yet another pep rally walk-through. Apparently the fire marshal had some problems with our Trojan Horse. Frustrated beyond belief by this point, I asked if I should bring a machete to cut through the red tape.

The updates I received from the battlefront let me know everything went according to our master plan. The Trojans rocked their buses back and forth as they pulled up to the restless crowd waiting for them outside Notre Dame Stadium. After exchanging "pleasantries" with several of our students, they pumped their fists along with the "BEAT SC!" chants that chased them down our tunnel onto our field. Though they tried to hide it, my friends assured me that our opponents looked at least a little unsettled. The battle had clearly begun, and we were already winning.

We bamboozled the fire marshal into approving our Trojan Horse as a temporary structure as long as he got to destroy it after the pep rally. That eliminated our chances of carrying it into the stadium like the students famously did before the 1977 "Green Jersey Game" when Notre Dame beat Southern Cal 49-19 on the way to a national championship. Oh, well. We hoped the football gods would award us for trying. I spent the rest of the day putting my efforts into something I could actually control. Setback after setback meant I had to deliver on my promise to give the students a "raw and unscripted Fightin' Irish War Rally." After running a few errands to a costume shop and a hardware store, I stopped by Alumni Hall's resident barber Adam Joines for a fresh cut. Then I snuck over to the Irish Green, climbed into the belly of the Trojan Horse, and waited to put on a show.

The Band of the Fighting Irish performed our traditional game-day songs while students from every dorm piled into the designated area set aside for them in front of the stage. I peered through the cracks in the wooden body of the giant horse, happy at what I saw. More students turned out to join our ranks than I had anticipated. They looked ready for battle as they moved into position under their various dorm flags like separate regiments of foot soldiers coming together to form one massive army. Most important, they all wore green.

When our band finished playing, Charles got on the mic to tell everyone that he couldn't find the Leprechaun so he would fill in until further notice. The last time anyone saw me, so he said, I was on a secret mission to steal Southern Cal's signature silver sword from their mascot, Tommy Trojan. A confused mutter sprang up from the crowd, so Charles gave the signal. The band kicked into our fight song and the cheerleaders pulled a large sheet aside to unveil our Trojan Horse. I waited for the chorus, popping out and standing on the monstrous horse's back right when everyone sang, "...loyal *sons* are marching onward to victory!"

Unsheathing the shiny chrome sword I bought at the costume shop a few hours earlier, I held it high for all to see. Tommy Trojan had a habit of raising his sword in a particular manner to the beat of whatever noise his band ineptly belched forth. I mimicked his motion for a few notes, and then I snapped the sword over my knee. The students rioted when I held the broken shards above my head. To top it all off, I pulled out the can of neon-green spray paint I picked up at the hardware store to tag the broad side of the plywood horse with the words "GO IRISH! BEAT SC!" While climbing onstage, I heard a girl in the front row of the student section yell out, "What the hell is going on? Who is this guy? This is freaking awesome!"

"Notre Daaame!" My two-word signature phrase sounded much better when the majority of my fellow students answered back. I tossed my hat aside and struck a pose while they marveled at my freshly shaved Mohawk.

"It's great to see all you *students* out here leadin' the charge tonight! And look at all you fans, too! I see you got the memo about wearing green. You look fabulous. Sadly, the Trojans are about to invade our campus with their ugly ketchup and mustard uniforms. Let's show 'em what real school colors look like when they get here. Our football players will take care of the blue and 24-karat gold. We need all of you to keep on reppin' the luck o' the Irish with more of my favorite color. Can you do that?" They sounded like they could.

"When Southern Cal steps onto *our* field, a sea of

green will be waiting for them. That's when they'll realize they aren't just goin' up against our football team.... No...They're goin' up against an entire united front of the Fightin' Irish Faithful!" The Fighting Irish Faithful let me know they liked their new nickname.

"When our boys in blue and gold get ready to take the field tomorrow, we need to give them a heroes' welcome with the classic 'Here come the Irish!' chant they used back in 1977. When the pre-game clock hits nine minutes, the fellas will start us off... Wait a minute, where are my manners? Let's have the ladies start us off with the echo chant. Ready for a practice run? Nine-oh-three, nine-oh-two, nine-oh-one, let's hear it!" The echo effect worked perfectly just as our players arrived. Everything was falling into place. I felt like the Leprechaun King of the World.

"Now I want you all to pay close attention, because I'm about to hand the mic over to a hero born behind enemy lines. That's right, he comes from Trojan territory. Let's see how much he learned from living in their midst. Hey, Jimmy! I have a few questions for you..." Jimmy Clausen took the mic from me hesitantly while the crowd cheered for their favorite California convert.

"Okay, we'll start off with an easy one: You know what USC stands for, right?" The students applauded his correct answer.

"That one was pretty standard. But, can you tell me when every Trojan football player experiences the best four years of his life?" He couldn't.

"Some might think it's during college but, for the Trojans, it's usually all four times they repeat their senior year of high school!" That one only got a pity laugh. I had to end on a high note.

"Okay, one last question: How many USC freshmen does it take to screw in a light bulb?" Again, he had no idea.

"Actually, that's a trick question. They don't take that class 'til sophomore year!" Another pity laugh—I decided to hang up my career as a standup comedian.

"Sorry 'bout that. Seriously though, Pete Carroll just announced that he only plans to dress thirty of his scholarship players for the game tomorrow. Do you believe that? I guess the rest of his players will have to get dressed all by themselves..." Finally, one the audience enjoyed. Content, I let the football players take over.

Jimmy kept it simple, saying he couldn't stand going home to hear everyone in Southern California talk smack so he planned to do something about it. Then co-captains Eric Olsen and Kyle McCarthy brought the latest edition of *The Observer* onstage to read the predictions written by our student sports reporters. All of them had picked Notre Dame to lose. Kyle shook his head in disbelief, and Eric invited any of those reporters who happened to be in attendance up onto the stage. No one answered his call. He looked out over the sea of students and fans dressed in green, saying he expected everyone to believe by game time and, if anyone had any more predictions they wanted to share with him, he would wait for them backstage.

With the mic back in my hand, I nervously introduced my favorite football player of all time: "I'm truly honored to welcome one of the most *electrifying* players to ever suit up in blue and gold. He used to make moves that left his opponents limping back across the field to go pick up their jockstraps after he raced his way into the end zone. He's got the moves, and he really is as fast as his name implies… Ladies and gentlemen, please welcome *Rocket Ismail*!"

Rocket took it to the next level with a deafening "WOOO! Let's get it!" Over the course of the next four minutes, he then proceeded to tear the house down. If our football players, students, and fans needed a spiritual revival, he gave them one they would never forget. Everyone in attendance turned to the person next to them on his command, saying, "Don't flinch!" Then everyone turned to the person on the other side to say, "Go get it!" Rocket made it clear that he didn't come to make us feel good. He only came to tell us the truth. Lucky for us, the truth would set us free. His advice: "Don't just give lip service to it. Make it a part of your fiber. Make it a part of your heartbeat." He told us that a challenge like the one we faced against Southern Cal required enough belief to surpass it. When he asked us if we believed, we came closer to actually shaking down the thunder than I had ever heard before. Satisfied, he spiked his mic against the stage with one final, "Don't flinch, and *go get it*!"

Sergio Brown picked the mic up from where Rocket dropped it, repeating, "Let's go get it! Let's go get it!" while his whole team mobbed their emotional leader. Multiple stage dives followed, so I caught the crowd-surfing wave over to my Dawgs where we linked arms for the Alma Mater. When I looked around at my Notre Dame Family swaying together as one, I finally felt it. We believed.

Game day technically began with our "Call to Arms Drum Circle" at midnight on the steps of the Golden Dome. I showed up in my Adidas high tops, rolled-up navy blue corduroys, a white shirt with the sleeves torn off, and bright green suspenders. The powers that be already deemed my Mohawk too scandalous to appear on national television during the game, so I made sure to enjoy my final hours before going bald. With my "Kill So. Cal" Irish Tricolour flag draped around my neck, I stood atop the pillar at the foot of the steps giving short but fierce wartime speeches through a bullhorn between drum cadences.

I had never seen so many fans at a midnight drum circle, so I turned it into a bonus pep rally for all those diehards who didn't want to let sleep interfere with "Beat SC Week." At one point, our "Gooo Irish! Beeeat Trojans!" chant grew so loud that hundreds of students came running out of their nearby dorms to join the mob. The drumline showcased perfect timing, per usual, when they ignited their cymbals with eerie green flames just as I started into my speech about the "Green Jersey Game" of 1977. The early morning air may have felt cold to some, but I was almost certain I could tell the exact moment when chills overtook our fans once they finally submitted to the hype.

Forcefully repeating Rocket's "Go get it!" mantra at every pre-game tailgate appearance I made, I finally lost my voice somewhere along the route of our Step-Off Parade. Then I had a "whoa" moment when I first saw the sea of green steadily streaming into our stadium before kickoff. Watching all those people respond to the passion I worked so hard to spread felt immensely empowering and humbling at the same time.

Crying became my favorite activity of the day. I couldn't control it. I had packed way too much emotion into this one event. My tears watered a 100-yard stretch of grass while I ran down our field with the extra-large blue, gold, and green flag donated by the Notre Dame Alumni Association for this special occasion. The football players followed me through a human tunnel formed by members of our Monogram Club. As I sprinted past heroes like Mike Brown, Reggie Brooks, and Rocket Ismail, I sobbed some more. Then my waterworks really let loose when both teams lined up for the opening kick. All that passion, all that hard work, all that hype, and all that belief came down to this.

☘

The Trojans torched us through the air. Matt Barkley connected on his first three passes and just like that we trailed 7-0. Everyone thought it, but I said it out loud: "Here we go again." I hadn't given up hope yet, but that miserable feeling of dread started to creep back into my mind. Then

Charlie Weis made a gutsy fake-field-goal call that went for 30 yards, and I thought the football gods just might smile down on us for the first time in a long while. Robert Hughes punched it in from three yards out to tie the score, and the students sounded off with their new favorite cheer: "Huuughes!"

Though we looked outmatched athletically at almost every position, our defense refused to back down. I stood on the sideline screaming at the top of my lungs before every defensive snap, enticing the students to test the limits of their vocal chords every third down by waving my arms wildly. The Trojan defense entrenched itself while ours bent dangerously close to the end zone. Still, we wouldn't break. It took a miracle, but we managed to remain within striking distance when the first half ended and we only trailed 13-7. I refused to leave the field during halftime. Instead, I ran furiously around the entire stadium to tell everyone how much we needed them to give us all they had left during the second half. I hoped at least a few of the fans watching me would see how much I cared. Maybe witnessing my passion would make some of them believe.

The Trojans scored again before anyone even knew the second half had started. Down 20-7, the faces around me started to reflect that doom and gloom attitude I hated more than anything. I tried to raise their spirits by keeping my chin up. Then Jimmy tossed a perfect deep ball to Golden, who came down with it despite tight double coverage by two of the most highly touted defensive backs in the nation. I made sure they both knew they couldn't handle Golden by getting in their faces as they sat in the end zone after the touchdown. One of them looked up at me and said, "Scoreboard." I responded with, "Don't call it a comeback, 'cause we're only down six!" An official pulled me off the field before we got too dicey, yelling, "Get out of here! You're not part of this game!" After pondering his words for a few minutes, I decided he was wrong. We were all part of this game.

The score didn't stay 20-14 for very long, but I still felt confident enough to tell Southern Cal's stud tight end not to get too comfortable as they kicked an extra point to go up 27-14. The throat slashing gesture he directed towards me would've landed him a hefty fine in the NFL. I reminded him how slow he was by getting the hell out of his way in a flash. As fate would have it, that same tight end burned our secondary a few minutes later to make the score 34-14. He even took the time to seek me out and stare me down after crossing the goal line. It couldn't end like this. Not after I worked so hard to make everyone believe. Not with my foot in my mouth. I asked Our Lady to bail me out just this one time. Then I prayed ten straight "Hail Marys" to atone for my trash-talking sins.

Jimmy answered my prayers by willing us back into the game. He scrambled on his one good foot to make big play after big play as he literally wrenched the momentum away from his fellow Californians. A quick score preceded a strong defensive stand, and we found ourselves back within striking distance. Another perfect touchdown pass from Jimmy to Golden ended with that same safety falling onto his back once again. This time I restrained myself from entering the field of play in order to avoid the officials who had their eyes on me. I couldn't have lived with myself after costing us the game with a penalty. It would have been the ultimate disgrace, worse than death for a Leprechaun. I bit my lip and clapped politely like everyone else.

Our defense gave us the ball back, down 34-27 with two minutes to go. I looked around while Jimmy broke the huddle to start the final drive, taking it all in. Without warning I resumed my uncontrollable crying. I didn't even know why or how it started, but I knew the powerful beauty of that moment would stay with me forever. The spirit of Notre Dame swallowed the whole scene, and it was a sight to behold.

Everyone believed, but no one could breathe as we drove the ball down to their four-yard line with just nine seconds left. It didn't matter who anyone was rooting for, we all contributed to one giant collective hyperventilation. The ball hung in midair for a century before it glanced off Kyle Rudolph's fingertips in the end zone on what looked like the last play of the game. Just an inch closer or a split-second sooner and we would've had ourselves an overtime shootout for the ages. Video review put four seconds back on the clock, but another incomplete pass left us with double zeros. Then, like a reverse version of that nightmarish game back in 2005, the officials extended the game by one more second. It looked like destiny at first, but we fell one play short when the ball sailed wide on Jimmy's last heave into the end zone. Smug smiles spread across the Southern Cal sideline.

My tears kept falling when I finally realized we just lost the one game I had put my entire heart into, but the anger and sadness I expected never came. Rather than hatred, love filled my field of vision. Everything seemed so immaculately bright as I looked up at my fellow students swaying arm in arm to our Alma Mater. I sent one final "Beat SC Week" letter that night:

> Dear Notre Dame Family,
>
> The recent realization that I will only serve as your Leprechaun for three more home games has me in a panic. Before I take my final steps on our hallowed field, I want to share the most important lesson I have taken away from my experience here at Notre Dame.
>
> Rocket told us "some legendary stuff" would take place when our Fighting Irish took on Southern Cal. He was right. I came out of our tunnel ready to be all that I could be for Notre Dame, our student section came out in full force like a loyal green army, and our team came ready to play like true champions.
>
> I shed quite a few tears while we fought back within yards of tying the game. They were not tears of sadness, but of joy as I stood in awe of that moment. When the game ended my tears continued, not out of disappointment, but due to pride. I had never felt more proud to be a student at Notre Dame than

I was when I stood facing the student section with tears streaking down my face while we all sang our Alma Mater together. I felt the spirit of Notre Dame at that moment, and I hope you all get to feel that way about something at some point in your lives.

Soak it all in, enjoy it, and let yourselves get swept away by the spirit. We forget so often what it feels like to truly live in the moment. Notre Dame has taught me that doing so with love and gratitude in my heart will fuel me with an energy I never knew I could possess. When it is all finally over, I hope I will have shared that lesson with as many members of my Notre Dame Family as possible.

Love thee Notre Dame,
Your Fighting Irish Leprechaun

Week Seven

Notre Dame Fighting Irish

vs.

Boston College Eagles

The Holy War

Notre Dame Stadium

Notre Dame, IN

Campus emptied quietly for fall break, as if slowly deflating from the thrills of "Beat SC Week." I went back to Buffalo so I could forget about football for a few days. Recuperating away from all the crowds turned out to be exactly what the doctor ordered. Still, I almost dreaded returning for the pep rally on Friday. I felt completely emotionally drained. The past several weeks of last-second escapes and near misses had taken its toll. Now I faced the daunting task of starting over after such a soul-crushing loss. This wasn't the way it was supposed to be.

Just when my will began to waver, the spirit of Notre Dame found a way to make me get up, brush the dirt off my shoulder, and keep fighting. The notes waiting for me upon my return reminded me why I loved life as the Notre Dame Leprechaun:

> Hello,
>
> I don't know if you remember this or not, but at the end of the ND vs. USC game you took a photo with a little fellow on the wall by the tunnel. You had just taken off your green Leprechaun

coat to put on your ND jacket. That was my son Trey. He is three years old, and it was his first game ever. I just want you to know how much that meant to him. He wanted to get his picture taken with you all day, but we missed you every time we tried to catch you. Thank you for taking time out of your day for him. He loves Notre Dame.

CPT Ronnie Matthews, US Army

Dear Sir,

You inspire us all, and we are indebted to your spirit. Thanks for everything you do. Go Irish!

Connor

To the Leprechaun,

Thank you for representing Our Lady's University the way you do. I share your love for Notre Dame, and I know exactly how you feel. Carry that spirit with you throughout your life. You will be amazed at all the wonder it brings. Go Irish!

Kelly

Mr. Leprechaun,

You are living the dream. Keep having fun, and enjoy your time at the most magical place on earth. We are all proud of you.

William

With a fresh look at the big picture provided by my extended Notre Dame Family, I found the motivation I needed to prepare for the upcoming pep rally. Even if we lost the rest of our games, my actions would still matter to so many people. Plus, with a 4-2 record we needed only two more wins to guarantee ourselves a free vacation during bowl week. Beating Boston College would bring us halfway there.

The more I planned for the weekend ahead, the more I looked forward to a perfectly timed visit from our favorite Catholic New Englanders. I grew up as an only child, but my best friend Drew's older brother Adam taught me that nothing feels better after getting beat up than the satisfaction that comes from pummeling your little brother. Previous generations of Domers referred to Boston College as "Fredo," in reference to Michael Corleone's inept younger sibling in *The Godfather*. Current Notre Dame students simply called our little brother school "Backup College." After enduring so much pain at the hands of our rival Trojans, the chance to raise our fists against our little brother would feel like a guilty pleasure. The only problem was the fact that we hadn't beaten them in six straight attempts. We would have to reclaim the right to call ourselves superior.

The promotions staff made me promise that I would adhere to a strict schedule after my antics at the Southern Cal pep rally. I thought they were joking at first, but they seemed rather serious at the walk-through when we rehearsed our entire show minute by minute. I wrote out a timing sheet to summarize their expectations so I wouldn't the first unemployed Leprechaun in history:

6:15 p.m. – Introduce Band Director Dr. Dye
6:30 p.m. – Introduce Football Team
6:35 p.m. – Introduce Ian Williams
6:40 p.m. – Introduce Golden Tate
6:45 p.m. – Football Team Exits (Alma Mater)
6:50 p.m. – Band Exits (Fight Song)

My enthusiasm cooled off a bit when the temperature dropped below zero and I took the stage in front of very few fans. No students showed up, so I focused my attention on the group of my family and friends huddled together up front. They looked excited for what would basically amount to a private pep rally for them, so I made the best of it. At only ten minutes past six, I was already ahead of schedule as well. If nothing else, I would make sure the promotions staff loved me by the end of the night.

"Notre Daaame! We have a big game against our little brother tomorrow afternoon, but we'll talk more about that later. Right now we're gonna set the tone in true Fightin' Irish fashion by welcoming the man behind the best damn band in the land…Dr. Dye!" Our band director explained the history behind our fight song, along with every other traditional tune our band would play on game day. He did a great job filling his allotted fifteen minutes, but the football team still hadn't arrived when he gave me the mic back. I crumpled up my timing sheet while thinking of ways to improvise.

"Thanks, Dr. Dye! Alright, ladies and gentlemen…" My mind went blank. The few people in the crowd whose names I didn't know looked restless and bored, or maybe just cold and shivering. Either way, I had no idea how long it would take the football team to show up. I contemplated either a long drawn-out explanation of the infinite ways we excelled above and beyond our littler brother, or just a few cheers until someone bailed me out. A bus filled with Backup College students unloaded behind the crowd, so I went with my first choice.

"Ladies and gentlemen... This is a *big game* for us, but not because it's a rivalry game. All those BC fans back there have been going around all week telling everyone how excited they are to visit their rivals at Notre Dame, but they're not our rivals. Hey, you in the back! Guess what! You're *not* our rivals!" A clean split formed between the Notre Dame fans laughing in the front and the Backup College fans booing in the back. I liked where this was headed.

"All you BC fans back there may *want* to be our rivals, but you can't ever have a true rivalry with your big brother..." The laugh/boo split grew more distinct. "...and we can't ever have a true rivalry with our little brother because no matter how hard he tries to be as big as us, or as tough as us, or as strong as us...no matter how much he aspires to be just like us...he's still our little brother...no matter what. The same goes for our little brother school up there in Massachusetts..." The Backup College fans outnumbered the Fighting Irish Faithful by this point, so I catered my speech to my audience. I pointed directly at them as I spoke.

"No matter what, we're still the big brother in this relationship. We're still Touchdown Jesus. We're still the Golden Dome. We're still Fr. Sorin, Fr. Hesburgh, and Fr. Rozum. We're still the Grotto and the Basilica. We're still Knute Rockne, the Four Horsemen, and Frank Leahy. We're still Ara Parseghian. We're still Dan Devine. We're still Lou Holtz. We're still seven Heismans and eleven national championships. We're still Gold and Blue through and through, and we're still *Notre Dame...no matter what!"* My speech came off as arrogant, but true. Everyone knew it, even our little brothers in the back. If they hadn't accepted my words as true, they wouldn't have reacted so negatively. My message hit home and I loved it. The reverse pep rally went on.

"That's not all, though... You see, as the big brother in this relationship, we have a tremendous responsibility to uphold. We must assert our superiority. We can't let our little brother even *think* he might have a chance at becoming the man of the house. We need to step up and make a statement...right here...right now...and that's where *you* come in." I pointed right at my family and friends. They backed me up willingly.

"It's simple, really. We got our hearts broken last week, but it's time to take it out on our little brother this week... You with me?" When I felt a tap on my shoulder, I thought the promotions staff had fired me right on the spot. Instead, they told me the football team had been waiting backstage for the past two minutes. I apologized for getting too worked up to remember my timing sheet, but I was secretly glad the team witnessed most of my angry rant.

"Now let's hear it for the men who will make our statement loud and clear on the field tomorrow...your 2009 University of Notre Dame Fightin' Irish!" The team took forever to get onstage, leaving us hopelessly behind schedule.

I worked quickly to get back in line with the timing sheet: "Our official football program describes our first speaker as 'the most powerful defensive player on the roster.' He's *the* foundation of our defense, and every time you see BC's offensive line collapse tomorrow I guarantee he'll be front and center... Please welcome our nose tackle, *Ian Williams*!" Ian thanked our fans for braving the cold to show their support, and then he guaranteed his defense would be ready to go by the next afternoon. He admitted the loss against SC left him hurting, but he promised to use that pain as motivation every time he lined up alongside his brothers on the defensive line. His straightforward sincerity won the crowd over, and even the Backup College fans in the back refrained from heckling him.

Golden Tate took his speech in a different direction altogether. When I asked him what BC really stood for, he surprised me by unzipping his track jacket to reveal the "Backup College" t-shirt he wore underneath. I pretended I had it planned out like that all along. He went on to tell all the Backup College fans in attendance that he looked forward to celebrating our upcoming win with them at CJ's Pub after the game. Then he compared their

Eagle logo to our Fighting Irish logo, telling "all the little birdies in the back row" to mind their manners and quiet down while he spoke. Ever the southern gentleman, he apologized while clarifying that his jokes were all in good fun. He didn't want to upset them until he burned their defense the following day.

Our band hurried through the Alma Mater so the football team could get out of there on time. Sick of dealing with the cold and the constraints of my timing sheet, I turned to go rather than stick around to chat with fans like usual. When an usher stopped me, I let out an exasperated, "What now?" He introduced me to an elderly woman peering up at me from her wheelchair with dozens of blankets wrapped around her. The usher told me she was a lifetime fan and this was her first time on campus. I said, "Welcome home!" to her without really thinking about it, but the single tear I saw fall from the corner of her eye down into her several layers of scarves stopped me in my tracks. More tears appeared, and her unexpected response jogged my memory. We talked for a few minutes, and then I honored my vow to make the most out of my position by welcoming many more new faces to the most magical place on earth.

The temperature warmed into the low teens on game day. The sight of students returning to campus, along with what we liked to call "relative warmth" in South Bend, reheated my enthusiasm as I roamed around making tailgate appearances. Some of the cheerleaders grumbled about wearing skirts in that kind of weather, but I actually took comfort in knowing that I wouldn't end up soaked in either sweat or rain by the end of the day.

Both teams looked frozen in place by the arctic blast taking place just prior to kickoff. Charles said he had never seen me bounce up and down so much at a game. I assured him the wind-chill had nothing to do with it. We hoped our offense would give us good reason to jump around some more, but two field goals and a safety later we found ourselves ahead 6-2 in a total snoozer. The first real fireworks of the game came when our little brother scored to go ahead 9-6. Then Jimmy found his favorite target to make it 13-9 before half. Golden tweeted like a "little birdie" as he ran past the Backup College Eagle mascot on his way up the tunnel. I held my hand out for a high-five when I jogged past the feathery fellow, pulling it away at the last second to the delight of our ushers standing nearby. When the Eagle took her head off backstage to reveal her long flowing hair, I felt bad for acting so impolitely to a nice young lady.

The second half began with little more to cheer about, especially when our little brother connected on a few big pass plays to go up 16-13. Skepticism started to squeeze its way into my thoughts, but Kyle McCarthy made sure we all got to celebrate by picking off his second pass of the game. Every time our defense forced a turnover, the band would play a cadence they called "Metallica." Whenever we heard that drum beat, all of the guy cheerleaders and I would start a mosh pit in the end zone until at least one of us got knocked down. Those guys were big, and I usually ended up in the grass. After Kyle's interception, I came away with white stripes from the lines in our end zone all over my green knickers.

I momentarily forgot about my frozen fingers and toes when Jimmy tossed yet another perfect touchdown to Golden and we went up 20-16. Still, like a true little brother, Backup College just wouldn't go away. They kept hanging on until the very end when Brian Smith finally iced the game with an interception deep in our territory. After warming back up with several extended minutes of jumping around and tweeting like a "little birdie," I stopped to pose for a photo with a few Gator Bowl representatives. They told me how much they looked forward to seeing me in Jacksonville after at least one more win. I could have sworn I saw them licking their chops at the thought of their TV ratings after six of our last seven games had come down to the final drive—not to mention the fact that they *knew* our fan base would gladly take a trip to balmy Florida during the holidays. I thanked them for their kind words, but I secretly wanted nothing to do with the Gator Bowl. With only two losses and a cupcake schedule the rest of the way, it was BCS or bust for the Fighting Irish.

Week Eight

#25 Notre Dame Fighting Irish

vs.

Washington State Cougars

Shamrock Series

Alamodome

San Antonio, TX

After we beat Backup College, I decided to resume the weekly routine I unwisely deviated from prior to our loss against Southern Cal. That meant I had to stay at Club Fever with the cheerleaders until last call on Thursday night, even though our flight left for San Antonio at 6 a.m. Friday morning. We celebrated to the fullest during "Fever-ween," the one Halloween party no Notre Dame student could afford to miss. When I got back to my room in Alumni Hall at 3:45 a.m., a ten-minute power nap sounded like a good idea. A little extra rest would certainly give me the energy I needed to pack my suitcase and make it to the bus on time at 4:20 a.m.

I woke up at 4:15 a.m. to twenty missed calls and thirty text messages from my teammate Christy. Then I heard her yelling up into my window from the quad down below. She didn't sound especially happy. At that point we had three minutes left to get on the bus. No sweat. I threw a wad of Adidas gear into my gym bag, folded my Leprechaun suit neatly on top, and doused myself with cologne to mask the musky scent of Fever-ween.

I made it halfway down the hall before I realized that I had no idea where my travel buddy Charles was. He finally answered his phone after I left about a dozen voicemails. I told him he better get out of bed unless he didn't want to travel with the cheerleading squad anymore. He chose the latter option, quitting right on the spot. Christy and I wouldn't have it, so we dragged our sleepy partner-in-crime all the way to the bus. The pungent aroma of Club Fever met us instantly when we climbed on board. Coincidentally, we weren't even the last to show up. We waited with the rest of our bleary-eyed squad until our final missing teammate arrived, still in costume from Fever-ween. Our cross-country expedition for the inaugural Shamrock Series home-away-from-home game was already off to a memorable start by the time we left campus at 4:45 a.m.

I thanked the Lord above for the wonders that came complimentary with our chartered direct flight to San Antonio as I hid my bloodshot eyes behind my brand new pair of green and black plastic sunglasses with "GO IRISH" printed on the side. Our all-inclusive luxury vacation continued when we checked into our stylish accommodations at the Westin La Cantera Hill Country Resort just outside San Antonio. After spending too much time napping and too much money on room service, we all congregated next to the grand piano in the lobby to receive our schedules and a daily cash allowance. Our busy travel itinerary included a trip to Fort Sam Houston, a pep rally in front of the Alamo, pre-game tailgate appearances downtown in the main plaza, a parade through the city streets, and finally a football game.

As the only proud Texan on our squad, the responsibility fell on Molly to teach us the lyrics of "Deep in the Heart of Texas." She instructed her drowsy students with impressive patience, and most of us had the words memorized by the time we reached Fort Sam Houston. While at the US Army base there, we had the honor of spending the afternoon with several severely injured soldiers and their families through the Wounded Warriors Project. A group of kids greeted us with green pompoms and a homemade poster that read, "Go Irish! Welcome ND!" They watched with admiration as the cheerleaders performed their stunts, and they promised they would tune in to the rest of our games on TV so they could point us out to their friends. I looked around at all the smiling faces, and that same feeling I got every time I swayed to the Alma Mater came back. We left feeling enormously humbled by the sacrifices those brave families had made for our freedom. Our bus fell silent as we all sat staring out the window, reflecting on the spirit we had just shared with some of America's finest heroes.

None of us could believe the number of people already packed into downtown San Antonio for our pep rally when we pulled up next to the Alamo. Fans dressed in Notre

Dame gear stretched as far as the eye could see, leaving no street, sidewalk, park bench, or patch of grass unoccupied. We all paused to marvel at the beautiful backdrop provided by the famous Alamo façade directly behind us, contrasted against the charming city streets straight ahead. Then we remembered we had a show to run. We took the stage and right away I could sense something different about these fans. They showcased their southwestern flair by clapping their hands, stomping their boots, hooting, and hollering along with us the whole time. The rally started to feel like a scene from an old Western film, and I half-expected several pistols to discharge celebratory shots up into the air when we danced to our band's rendition of "Deep in the Heart of Texas."

After the show, we got mauled by thousands of the most dangerously eager Fighting Irish fans I had ever seen. Every time I posed for a photo, another fan would yank me in the opposite direction and I would pose again. Rather than neat and orderly lines, I found myself in the middle of a Wild West showdown. Following each barrage of camera flashes, several hands shot out to offer me sturdy handshakes before wrenching me around towards their friends and family. When I finally made it through the crowd without getting hogtied or dragged away by a lasso, I thanked our animated hosts for sharing their inspiring enthusiasm. They promised to keep it up for the rest of the weekend.

Game day began a little differently as well. Once my teammate Chris and I counted up the cash we had left over from our previous night of endless authentic burritos and margaritas, we settled on a suitable way to spend the rest. The attentive staff at our lavish resort spa pampered us like kings, and they even let us wear our fluffy white bathrobes out to the winding river pool after our full body massages. A few hours of sipping agave nectar iced tea and lounging in the southwestern sun got us in the right frame of mind for some Fighting Irish football.

An afternoon spent making celebrity appearances throughout downtown San Antonio all but drained us, but we savored every second we spent with its genuinely ecstatic citizens in their hot, sticky, crowded streets. I appreciated the Tex-Mex twist they added to the typical Notre Dame home-game experience. All of our normal game-day activities went according to plan, but the mob surrounding us in the main plaza nearly tore me limb from limb when I didn't move fast enough for more photos. Charles and Mike had to pull double Leprechaun duty just to make sure I survived.

Our Step-Off Parade stretched from the San Fernando Cathedral across town to the Alamodome over a mile away. The good people of San Antonio continued to embrace our presence in impressive fashion by lining the entire route. The trek left all of us entirely exhausted, except for our teammate Kaitlyn who amused the crowds by continuing to march past the stadium in a one-man parade of her own after failing to realize our band had stopped playing. Her sideshow solidified her status as a fan favorite, and every teenage boy in sight instantly had a new crush.

A father and his young son approached me with a football covered in signatures when we arrived outside the Alamodome. They told me about the pilgrimage they had made to Notre Dame several years before, and their plans to go back when they could afford a return trip. In their words, they "ate, breathed, and slept" Notre Dame during every football season. Even more important, they loved everything our school stood for as a Catholic university committed to doing good throughout the world. I felt unfit to pen my name alongside such signatures as those of Ara Parseghian, Lou Holtz, Brady Quinn, and Jeff Samardzija, but they assured me that my mark would provide the luck they needed to see the Golden Dome again one day. When I thanked them for making me feel important, the father looked me straight in the eye to tell me how much my enthusiasm shaped his son's dreams. His words left me more or less speechless, but I managed to share one final "Go Irish!" with both of them before following the cheerleaders into our new home field.

Thousands of Leprechauns stared back at me when I led the football team out onto the field inside the Alamodome. Some of their Halloween costumes came close to rivaling my own Leprechaun suit, and I even saw a few good Lou Holtz impersonators, but the row of Our Lady look-alikes—dressed from head to toe in glittery gold—stole the show. As if our fans in San Antonio hadn't impressed me enough by that point, they generated more noise inside their stadium than I had ever heard at any football game. They wasted no time making sure they provided us with a true home-field advantage prior to kickoff. Unfortunately, their noise level peaked when our offense took the field. The excited roar that followed our first play from scrimmage never died down, and Jimmy Clausen had a hard time calling audibles during our entire opening possession. We appreciated their collective effort nonetheless, and they eventually managed to hold their voices back until our defense took the field.

I finally got to put my feet up and enjoy a game that didn't come down to the last play, as our boys in blue and gold took care of Washington State with relative ease. Our 40-14 victory made for a fitting conclusion to a weekend filled with good vibes, celebration, and relaxation. Golden Tate dominated yet again with 80 yards receiving, 60 more rushing, and a gratuitous Hail Mary touchdown reception over three defenders just before the first half ended. The video board showed that play on loop during halftime, and everyone got a kick out of the confidence I showed when I raised my arms to signal for a touchdown while the ball was still in the air well before he wrestled it away from all three defenders.

Determined to celebrate like locals, the cheerleaders and I went on a quest for some tequila back at our resort. We figured it was late enough at night and we were far enough away from downtown that no fans would recognize us at the poolside lounge, but as soon as we walked in we received a standing ovation in honor of the Fighting Irish. Discovered but undeterred, we took our private party outside to a table off by itself. Our stealthy merrymaking made us proud at first, until several salt-dipped glasses of the finest distilled agave came our way courtesy of the Notre Dame fans seated inside. We decided to give in and spend the rest of the night singing "Deep in the Heart of Texas" under the big bright stars spread across the wide and high prairie sky.

Week Nine

#19 Notre Dame Fighting Irish
vs.
Navy Midshipmen

Notre Dame Stadium
Notre Dame, IN

The excitement that came with gaining bowl eligibility gave way to a deep sinking feeling when we lost to Navy for the second time in a row at home. After taking care of our classic rivals without any real scares for 43 straight years, the longest winning streak in NCAA history between annual opponents, we had just inexplicably dropped two out of our last three games in the series. Our distressing 23-21 loss to the Midshipmen knocked the wind right out of our sails just as we thought our team had caught another wave of momentum. No one knew how to react. We all just stood around scratching our heads and staring blankly at the bleak aftermath of the shipwreck we had just witnessed.

Just two weeks before, "BCS or bust" became our unofficial slogan as an obvious buzz returned to campus. It had taken a tremendous amount of time and effort to build that buzz, but it all went away in a flash. The loss left South Quad looking like an eerily quiet ghost town on Monday morning, and I waited for tumbleweeds to blow by while I sat down on a bench outside Alumni Hall to read all about it in *The Observer*. I hesitantly flipped to the sports section only to find a photo of myself standing with my hands on my hips and my mouth agape in disbelief. The headline read, "Campus shocked after Navy's upset."

Rather than torture myself by reading the undoubtedly depressing text that accompanied my mug shot, I took a walk around Saint Mary's Lake to clear my mind. Her shimmering waters always helped me reflect on my life from a different angle. When I thought back to the game, I focused on the beautiful pageantry of our traditional rivalry, the moment of silence to honor those who had given the ultimate sacrifice to serve our country, the Navy officer who directed our band during the National Anthem, and the thunderous flyover provided by Navy's Blue Angels Squadron. Each of those moments stood as a blessing and a reminder of the honorable missions that linked Navy and Notre Dame.

I came to appreciate the unbreakable bond between my school and the Naval Academy when I wrote my senior thesis in Irish Studies about the true meaning of the words "Fighting Irish." Through my research, I learned that we cemented our brotherhood with Navy during World War II when the draft depleted our enrollment numbers so deeply that we came dangerously close to closing our doors for good. Navy bailed us out by sending thousands of midshipmen to attend classes and train on our campus throughout the rest of the war. Naval trainees comprised over 85 percent of our student body when our football team won a national championship in 1943. They even kept us afloat when we lost most of our star football players and coaches to the draft. After the war those coaches and players returned, attracting more applicants than ever before to join their ranks at Notre Dame. Not by coincidence, the golden era sparked by Navy's rescue mission encompassed our national championship seasons in 1946, 1947, and 1949. It also set the stage for our revived commitment to academic excellence as the nation's premier Catholic university.

Without the Naval Academy, the spirit of Notre Dame would have faded into obscurity during World War II. The dreams of Sorin and Rockne would have diminished into nothing more than distant echoes of a long-forgotten era. Leahy, Bertelli, and Lujack wouldn't have given new meaning to the words All-American. Parseghian, Devine, and Holtz wouldn't have recaptured the magic years later. Fr. Hesburgh wouldn't have changed the world from his seat as our president for 35 miraculous years. None of us would have gotten a chance to witness the feeling we fell in love with all over again every game day.

Even with such thoughts aiding my perspective, I just about wanted to crawl into a hole and die after our demoralizing loss. My misgivings almost infected my mind. Then the spirit preserved by Navy all those years ago confronted me once again. Another perfectly crisp and sunny

November day came to South Bend. A family from the Hannah & Friends Neighborhood called me to ask if I would dress up as the Leprechaun for their Christmas card portrait. Their sons struggled at times with special needs, but nothing cheered them up like visiting Notre Dame. They looked sharp in their matching white Aran wool sweaters when I met them at Main Circle. We spent an hour or so laughing while we talked about everything except football during our photo shoot in front of the Golden Dome. When I pointed out Alumni Hall, they asked how many of my little Leprechaun friends lived there with me. I asked them to keep my hiding spot secret, and then I let them in on my stash of lucky gold coins. They gave me cheerful high-fives when we shared one final "Go Irish!" before going our separate ways.

Our loss to Navy didn't seem so bad once I remembered the deeper meaning behind everything I stood for. Life as the Notre Dame Leprechaun wasn't just about winning football games. Winning definitely mattered, and the accomplishments of our football program stood as one of the most powerful influences on the success of our University. Yet, the power of Notre Dame had always extended well beyond the gridiron. As a representative of that power, I had the ability to change lives each and every day. I considered my own life as a direct loan from God, and I planned to repay it with interest.

Week Ten

Notre Dame Fighting Irish
vs.
#8 Pittsburgh Panthers

Heinz Field
Pittsburgh, PA

In just one week we dropped out of the national rankings, lost out on any shot we had at a BCS Bowl, and became a nationwide laughingstock. With absolutely nothing left to lose, I decided it was about time to shake off the after-effects of that Navy game with some good old-fashioned fun in the Steel City. After a quick interview with the *Pittsburgh Tribune-Review* on Thursday night, I hit the hay early to rest up for the adventures that lay ahead.

The cheerleaders and I departed by bus early Friday morning, arriving in time for lunch at our teammate Craig's house, located in the picturesque rolling hills of southwestern Pennsylvania. We enjoyed a delicious home-cooked meal with his parents before making our way downtown, where the Notre Dame Club of Pittsburgh impressed us with their professionally run pep rally at Station Square. All we had to do was show up and look pretty. They took care of the rest. I met several families who appreciated my Rust Belt roots, and they generously shared some of Pittsburgh's finest delicacies with us. Their zesty Kielbasa pork sausage and salad topped with thick stacks of cheesy french-fries gave me the extra kick I needed to teach everyone the authentic Leprechaun Jig. As much as they loved their city, they obviously took just as much pride in representing Notre Dame. After the rally, we kept their recommendations in mind as we hit the vibrant local restaurant scene.

Fat, happy, and tired, we almost called it a night when we returned to our hotel at 11 p.m. Then we remembered our football team didn't play until the following evening, so we made a group decision to rally for a much-needed night out on the town. After all, our midnight curfew was more of a guideline than a rule. We hashed out a plan, and then I almost blew it when I attempted to stroll right out the front door while carrying a bottle of Yuengling. Several upper-level members of our administration who were holding a powwow in the main lobby politely asked where I was off to as I sauntered by in my favorite pair of jeans and a freshly ironed button-down shirt. The improvisational skills I had picked up as the Leprechaun kicked in at a moment's notice, and I pointed to the hotel convenience store without even having to verbalize an excuse. Fifty cents and a pack of gum later, I took the elevator up to the second floor and walked back down a different set of stairs to a fire exit out back.

One close call led to another when our Pittsburgh native tour guide Craig almost convinced us to trust the sketchy-looking character who offered us a ride wherever we wanted to go in his big white van with no windows for only $20. Luckily, my friend Keegan who had just finished his service with the Marines met up with us at just the right moment. He charitably paid our cab fare in return for the once-in-a-lifetime chance to party behind enemy lines with the Notre Dame cheerleaders.

Unfortunately, the bouncers throughout Pitt's bar district didn't treat us as kindly as our new bodyguard Keegan. We called her Baby Kate for obvious reasons, but we had a hard time understanding why none of the bars would admit our particularly tiny teammate despite her three different forms of identification. Not willing to give up so easily, we settled for a house party hosted by some Pitt frat boys who knew Craig. As expected, we caused quite a stir when we walked in the door. My big mouth didn't stay shut for too long either. Before we knew it, we found ourselves in the middle of a Notre Dame versus Pitt flip-cup contest to decide which side got bragging rights for the rest of the night.

Down three games to two in the seven-game series, I asked for a rule clarification prior to our pivotal game six. Our hosts surprisingly agreed with my interpretation, but the frat boy standing directly across the warped wooden table from me continued to cheat anyway. I took matters into my own hands by swatting his red Solo cup away. Someone retaliated by throwing an unopened can of Natty Ice at me from across the room. Rather than hit me, the can connected with a cup positioned in front of my teammate Chris. An ill-fated bounce sent the contents of that cup splashing onto his very fashionable, very white, very stainable shirt.

As the biggest guy at the party, Chris didn't hesitate to flip the entire table over in response to the outrageously inhospitable act committed by our hosts. Everyone froze, the music came to a screeching halt, and I began to silently count out how many of our potential adversaries I thought would actually jump us. We were outnumbered at least ten to one, but Keegan gave us a military-trained secret weapon in disguise. I liked our odds, but I couldn't stop picturing myself on national television the next night with a black eye and a missing tooth. That wasn't a look I felt like explaining to the members of our administration who I had come across just a few hours earlier. With no other options presenting themselves, I improvised with a "USA! USA! USA!" chant as we slowly backed our way towards the door. Thankfully, the frat boys at Pitt were far more patriotic than they were hospitable.

Still not ready to stop partying, but growing wary of the whole Pitt scene, we searched for a bar closer to our hotel. The Souper Bowl gave us exactly what we were looking for. We owned the place and the gracious bartender even let us stay after hours when he closed it off to outside business. He happened to be a Fighting Irish fan, so we tried to make his slow night memorable by chatting with him until the sun came up. When it came time to pay our tab, we noticed several rounds mysteriously missing from the long list of cocktails we had sampled. He insisted that he hadn't made a mistake when we brought the omissions to his attention. We thanked him for his generosity, and he wished us luck against Pitt. In his words, most "real Pittsburghers" would take the Fighting Irish over the Panthers any day.

We enjoyed our sightseeing tour along the rivers and up the Duquesne Incline while trying to rehydrate throughout the following afternoon. Then we suited up and assembled in the hotel lobby with the Pittsburgh Bureau of Police officers who would escort us to the game. They surrounded our bus with squad cars and motorcycles, literally stopping city traffic with their blaring sirens and flashing lights as we sped through a maze of bridges towards Heinz Field. More excellent food and friendly faces awaited us at the Notre Dame Club of Pittsburgh pre-game pep rally outside Clark Bar & Grill, where we chanted and jigged in anticipation of our soon-to-come victory.

The Pitt student section lined both sides of the tunnel inside Heinz Field, which made for an interesting entrance as I led the charge through a heavy downpour of bottles, cans, food wrappers, and saliva. The stadium itself looked imposing with black and yellow everywhere and two gargantuan Heinz Ketchup bottles that lit up bright red every time Pitt scored. A giant video board added to their home-field advantage as well, but they could have gone without the irritating piped-in panther growl sound effects after every first down.

Missed tackles by our defense caused that maddening growling noise to play on repeat for most of the first half. Pitt's stud running back, Dion Lewis, tore through our failed arm tackles so easily that he made it sound like panther mating season had arrived. The outcome looked bleak when we trailed by double digits late in the second half, but Golden Tate took his cue to dominate the game by fighting his way into the end zone and then taking a punt 87 yards to the house less than a minute later. Our regular punt returner had lined up in his normal position prior to the play, but Golden waved him off the field so he could take over by bursting right up the middle through defenders with a lightning bolt of speed and power. He had a knack for coming through in the clutch like that, but even his heroics couldn't save us from poor officiating. Down 27-22 with a chance to knock off the #8-ranked team in the nation on our final drive, we fell victim to a controversial fumble call that sealed our fate by giving the ball back to the Panthers. They made sure to thank every official for the assist as they walked out with a win.

A small group of Pitt fans made a weak attempt at storming the field when the Panthers finally ran out the clock. One of them swiped the Leprechaun hat right off my head as he ran by. My football instincts kicked in and I caught up to him, taking him down right before he reached the tunnel. With his face in the turf and my foot planted squarely on the middle of his back, I reached down to retrieve my now-misshapen Kelly green bowler. When I looked up, I saw a family of Pitt fans staring at me with their mouths wide open in amazement. I apologized for subjecting their kids to such violence, lifting my foot to let the perpetrator scamper away. To my surprise, the father thanked me for subjecting his sons to such a fine example of a properly executed form tackle. We all took a group photo together, and I congratulated them on their win.

The only other bright spot of the game, besides finally getting to savor more than our fair share of Primanti Bros. sandwiches at halftime, came when we met a man who introduced himself as Johnny Lattner's cousin. He told us that he wished he could accomplish as much as Johnny had for Notre Dame, but he tried to do all he could by volunteering in his community nonetheless. I told him that I believed we were all called to contribute in our own way, and I thanked him for adding to our mission. My words didn't sound especially profound when they left my lips, but he reacted as if I had just bestowed some great seed of wisdom upon him. He thanked the cheerleaders and me for making him feel included, and his response reminded me why I loved calling myself part of the Notre Dame Family.

Week Eleven

Notre Dame Fighting Irish
vs.
Connecticut Huskies

Senior Day

Notre Dame Stadium

Notre Dame, IN

"Students disappointed as Irish lose again" wasn't the headline I had in mind when I looked forward to celebrating my last game as the Leprechaun inside Notre Dame Stadium. By this point, most of our fan base had embraced a doom and gloom defense mechanism that I couldn't penetrate even with the most delusional optimism I could summon. To combat the sense of helplessness clouding my mind, I visited some of the only fans I knew I could still reach no matter how many losses blighted our record.

Carpal tunnel syndrome set in around autograph 731, a small price to pay for the wholesome sense of wonder that filled the local South Bend elementary school when every boy and girl got their own signed glossy Leprechaun photo. I wasn't exactly qualified to teach them about the specific dangers of doing drugs, but they all listened intently as a mythical fairytale creature told them to surround themselves with good people and set positive goals. When I sensed that my message might have been flying over their heads just a bit, I stuck with my training by turning the slogan of their drug awareness week into a cheer. The gym echoed with the sound of "Too smart…to start!" over and over until everyone found the courage to join in. The uplifting lack of negative football-related comments during our question and answer session made me more than happy to field endless inquiries about the details of rainbows, four-leaf clovers, and hidden pots of gold. I left feeling refreshed and ready to prepare for my final pep rally.

Maybe those kids were wise beyond their years, but the elegantly simple way they reacted to my visit launched me into a daylong reflection about life as the Notre Dame Leprechaun. I realized that my existence as such a powerful symbol included an intricate combination of awareness and confidence. Successfully wearing that green suit required the ultimate sense of self-assurance, but it also demanded the ability to overcome my ego entirely. As the Leprechaun, I had to rise above the feelings of insecurity and anxiety that tended to accompany uncertainty while simultaneously harnessing that very same nervous energy. The only way to find success in such an endeavor was to stop looking for it. Thinking about how others would judge me as I pranced around in front of 81,000 people while wearing goofy green knickers would only lead to self-induced paralysis. Letting go of all that useless noise freed me of my inhibitions, allowing me to truly live in every moment. Life as the Notre Dame Leprechaun was all about focusing on the love within those moments and sharing it with others. That was the gift.

☘

Ready to make the most out of my last chance to connect with my Notre Dame Family through a pep rally, I set to work planning out a show worthy of christening the newly renovated Joyce Center. Then I got the call from promotions. They insisted on keeping it at the Irish Green. The students had already expressed their distaste for that venue very publicly, but I knew there was nothing any of us could do about it. I felt bad for the seniors who would refuse to attend their last pep rally based purely on principal, and I shared the frustrations of the senior pom squad girls who had to grin and bear it as the routine they worked so hard to perfect got cut from the dreaded timing sheet. Talks of a walkout demonstration orchestrated by the entire student body started to surface, but I begged everyone to come together in honor of our senior class.

Hardly any students answered my pleas for solidarity, but those who did made me proud to stand up on that stage as their representative. I went with an extra-long, extra-personal introduction:

"Notre Daaame! Welcome to our senior game pep rally! We still have a few minutes 'til we get to bring our senior football players onstage, so I'm gonna take this time to sign off as your 2009 Notre Dame Football Leprechaun. You've all made this season into the most memorable year of my life, and I want to thank you." Their slow clap turned into a standing ovation. Since I was already standing, I tipped my Leprechaun hat and kept going.

"I'm not sure how many of you know me personally, but as a proud Irishman I always keep my family close to my heart. To all my family members watching from back home in Buffalo, my mom, my dad, my uncle Mark and his four boys Cyle, Layne, Logan, and Cayden, and my good friends from the Moran family who are right up here in the front row: Thanks for being here with me tonight." Most of them followed my lead by tipping their own caps to the crowd.

"This is it! This is our last rally. This one is for all you believers out there who will never give up on the Fightin' Irish…and it's for all my fellow seniors who are about to experience their last game in our student section." This time the few seniors standing by the stage tipped their caps as the crowd applauded.

"Ask any one of us seniors to describe our experiences inside Notre Dame Stadium, and I guarantee we have trouble putting the whole glorious spectrum of emotions we've felt into words. I found it nearly impossible when I sat down to write out how I feel, but here goes my best shot." I unfolded a sheet of paper covered with the words I had written down the night before:

"Big salty tears rolled down to my chin as I stood on the field during the fourth quarter of our football game against Southern Cal. I thought of my family and friends who joined millions more throughout the nation as they watched the final seconds tick away on TV. This momentous event represented so much more than a game to so many people and, as it came to a close, my tears continued. I got completely caught up in the overwhelming emotion of that moment, and I let it show as I faced the entire student section while we all sang our Alma Mater together as one. The Fighting Irish had lost, but they had fought until the very end. The inseparable connection I felt with everyone in the student section and the rush of pride I felt as a representative of Notre Dame hit me in a way that I will never forget. As I shuffled slowly back through the tunnel after hours of running and cheering until I could barely walk or speak, I knew I would remember how I felt at that moment for the rest of my life.

What I encountered inside our stadium on that pure Michiana autumn afternoon was the full force of the Notre Dame spirit hitting me all at once. The bond shared by every member of our Notre Dame Family is more than enough to bring anyone to tears. There is something special about this place that cannot be conveyed through words alone, but must be felt. It comes from our tradition, our pursuit of excellence in everything we do, and the respect that goes along with the name we have made for ourselves. Most importantly, it lives on through the people that make up our Notre Dame Family. Together, we carry out a mission that stands as a symbol of hope for so many…"

I couldn't make it through everything I wanted to say without getting choked up, so I cut myself short: "Thank you all. I honestly mean it when I call you my family. We are...Notre Dame!" A momentary pause ushered in a "WE ARE ND!" chant. The senior football players had already made their way onto the stage at some point during my speech, and they joined in with the rest of the crowd. We had been through a tiresome roller-coaster ride of a season together, but the sight of everyone clapping in unison made me believe we would eventually come out on top.

"Please allow me to introduce our senior class of football players who have instilled passion, toughness, and a never-say-die attitude into their team this year. You won't find a harder working group of tough gentlemen. They live up to their title as loyal sons of Our Lady, and they've sacrificed so much in her honor over the past four years. Give it up for *my* fellow seniors, and *our* class of 2010 Fightin' Irish!" Starting with their leader Sergio Brown, our seniors took a bow as the Fighting Irish Faithful voiced their appreciation.

"Since this is the last rally of the year and we're honoring all of our seniors tonight, I'm gonna kick it over to my man Bryan Hayes to do the rest of the intros. He's *the* lead senior football manager here at Notre Dame. Unfortunately, he plays hockey for Zahm Hall...and he did have to live through a humiliating defeat at the hands of the Alumni Dawgs last season...but I respect him greatly for being the man behind the scenes who gets it done for the Fightin' Irish day in and day out. Everybody please give it up for the one and only Brian Hayes!" Brian took over the pep rally, introducing the senior football players one at a time by telling embarrassing stories that had everyone rolling on the floor with laughter. He wasn't exactly an easy act to follow with my next introduction.

"When people ask me about my favorite Notre Dame Football players of all time, I usually start rattling off names like Rockne, Bertelli, Lujack, The Rocket, The Bus, and John Ryan. It's impossible to pick just one, but I do always mention our next speaker as well. He's as witty on his talk show as he is strong in his loyalty to Notre Dame. He holds his own on a network that usually loves to hate us, and he always represents his Alma Mater with class. Please welcome Mr. Mike Golic!" I expected Mike to talk our ears off after hearing him on the radio so often, but he kept his speech short. Turning to the football players, he told them to go out there and leave those fans who still believed with something to remember them by. Addressing the whole class of 2010, he said he hoped we would all enjoy our last game as students inside Notre Dame Stadium because we would remember it for the rest of our lives.

☘

My last game day on campus as the Notre Dame Leprechaun got off to a fine start when I woke up to some much-appreciated words of encouragement in the form of fan mail:

> Dear Dan,
>
> I just want to let you know that you're the most inspiring Leprechaun I can remember. I appreciate everything you do. Please keep it up. You're hands

down the king of mascots. Enjoy inspiring our home crowd one last time. No matter what happens today you will always be a champion in our eyes.

Thank you my friend,

Anthony

Dan,

As a Notre Dame fan who sat within yelling distance of your antics during every home game this year, I would like to thank you for all your cheering, dancing, and general rah-rahing over the course of the season. Enjoy your senior game.

GO IRISH!

Andy

The good vibes kept rolling in when I received a phone call from my munificent mentor, Father Jim McDonald. He wished me well, and then offered me six tickets in the section of golden seats down by the field along the 50-yard line for my family. I told him that I would never be able to thank him enough for his kindness, but he insisted that it was the least he could do for the most dedicated Notre Dame fanatic he had ever met. He wished me well once again, saying goodbye with a "God bless," which was always a good sign when it came from a Holy Cross priest.

Lots of lasts filled the rest of my day. I never thought six tiny girls could go through so many extra-large boxes of tissues, but the cheerleaders pulled it off with ease after our last tailgate appearance, our last Step-Off Parade, our last time warming up stunts inside Notre Dame Stadium, and especially our last charge through the tunnel ahead of the football team. In addition to her golden tickets, my mom got an all-access pass for the day. She captured most of our lasts through the lens of her camera, and I loved that I got to share such a significant day with her.

Our team looked like they wanted to go out with a bang when they put up 14 points in the first five minutes of the game. Then our energy fizzled out just like the hopes of our season. I tried to forget the frustration and simply enjoy my last game in the house that Rock built, but I found it tough to stand by and ignore the fact that our offense forgot how to score and our defense forgot how to tackle the far-from-fierce Connecticut Huskies. The biggest highlight took place during halftime when the cheerleaders and I joined the traditional senior class marshmallow fight in the student section. After I got blasted right between the eyes by an unseen sniper, I ran up the sticky stairs to crowd surf with my fellow Dawgs. Clumps of marshmallows clung to my knickers for the rest of the afternoon.

I enlisted the women's basketball team to help me wave Connecticut's potential game-winning field goal wide right from the front row, but we couldn't prevent our eventual 33-30 loss in double overtime. The Huskies ended our senior game by scoring right in my face as I stood in the back of the end zone. Then their whole team rushed the field to celebrate directly in front of our student section. It wasn't supposed to end like that. Senior day should have felt like a celebration, not a punch in the gut. We all stood around in stunned silence, not wanting to leave the field but not wanting to prolong the pain of watching those damn Huskies celebrate either. The cheerleaders cried a river that could have drowned the whole stadium, but for some reason I didn't feel sad. I just felt empty. It was all over, but it hadn't hit me yet.

Week Twelve

Notre Dame Fighting Irish vs. Stanford Cardinal

Battle for the Legends Trophy

Stanford Stadium

Palo Alto, CA

I hated myself for reading yet another depressing article when I opened up *The Observer* to the words: "Broken record: same old story as Irish lose another heartbreaker on senior night." The good old days when our record stood at 4-1 and then 6-2 were long gone. At 6-5, we could already sense that our game at Stanford would be the last for our head coach Charlie Weis. That meant we probably wouldn't go to a bowl game, either. I remained on my best behavior all season long just so I could finally get into a mascot fight with the whole world watching during bowl week. Maybe it wasn't meant to be. I still had one shot at instigating a brawl but, even with all my pent-up frustration, I knew I would feel bad taking down the defenseless Stanford Tree. He didn't even have arms.

Our season was a double-edged sword. Every game other than our blowout wins over Nevada and Washington State came down to the very last possession. It made for exciting football, but it also filled us with that dreadful sensation of coming so close while somehow remaining so far away. Our five losses only tallied up to a 21-point deficit overall. Just three more touchdowns worth of points over the course of our entire season, and we would be playing Stanford for a shot at our twelfth national championship. Instead, it looked like we had little to play for other than our own self-respect. Still, I couldn't have been more proud of the way our boys in blue and gold fought to the bitter end of every game. They shook off injuries, overcame adversity, and never stopped believing. I admired Charlie Weis for instilling that attitude in his team, and I hoped his career at Notre Dame could end with one last win in sunny California.

The cheerleaders and I boarded our chartered flight to San Francisco on Thanksgiving morning, arriving to the most gratifyingly extravagant feast I had ever laid eyes on. Notre Dame really outdid itself with the unlimited helpings of turkey, mashed potatoes, stuffing and gravy of all kinds, Alaskan king crab legs, jumbo shrimp, lobster tails, and oceans of cranberry sauce they laid out on our tables. The cheerleader guys stacked plate upon plate until they could stack no more. Then they spent the next two days digesting their meals while enjoying everything the beautiful City by the Bay had to offer. The girls made me take photos of them stunting in front of the Golden Gate Bridge, on the notorious prison island of Alcatraz, and even while holding bowls of clam chowder at Fisherman's Wharf.

Finally relieved of my duties as their cameraman, I enjoyed returning to my usual emcee role at the pep rally put on by the Notre Dame Club of San Francisco. The always-warm Northern California members of our Notre Dame Family welcomed us with open arms and mellow vibes that almost made me want to put a flower in my hair.

Game day began when Charles and I snuck out of the hotel after our midnight curfew to cause mayhem on Stanford's campus. We didn't mean any real harm, and we would certainly never do anything to deface such a beautiful place, but we did leave our mark by quoting *The Little Rascals* on every chalkboard we could find:

> Dear Stanford Nerds,
> We hate your stinking guts. You make us vomit. You're the scum between our toes.
> Love, Notre Dame

The $40 raw salmon pizza our luxury hotel force-fed us for breakfast did little to satisfy our stretched-out stomachs so soon after Thanksgiving. Luckily, the Notre Dame Club of San Francisco supplemented our diet with burgers, brats, and delectably creamy clam chowder at the pep rally they held right outside Stanford Stadium. I had never seen a football field surrounded by palm trees before, but it made sense when I finally came across the most ridiculously absurd mascot of all time. Stanford's Tree looked like a homemade prop from a high school musical, and he acted accordingly. Too many alcohol-related offenses committed by inebriated Trees over the years forced Stanford to adopt a new rule requiring all mascots to pass a Breathalyzer test prior to entering their stadium. Good thing I left my Jameson at home. Double zeros gave me the green light to leave it all on the field one last time.

The Fighting Irish came to battle. Helmet-cracking hits and pinpoint passes from Jimmy Clausen to Kyle Rudolph, Michael Floyd, and Golden Tate had us leading most of the game. Then Toby Gerhart changed all that by grinding up our defense for three touchdowns on the ground and one more through the air. I never wanted to run out onto the field and tackle a player more than I did that night. Good thing I didn't, because he probably would have stomped the life out of me with the tree trunks he called legs.

Stanford's joke of a band tried to taunt me during their halftime show, but I sent the tuba player who got too close stumbling backwards when I went after him with a raised shillelagh. We trailed in the second half, but stayed true to form by keeping the fans glued to their seats with one last final-second attempt at redemption. An unanswered Hail Mary left us with a 45-38 loss, an unemployed head coach, and cancelled flights to Jacksonville during Bowl Week. I spent our whole red-eye flight back to South Bend contemplating the ups and downs of our season. Somewhere between those highs and lows I had mastered the ability to share my dreams with others as I lived them out publicly. No tragic losses or disgruntled fans could ever take that away from me. The cheering and booing would eventually fade away, but the spirit, the struggle, and the triumph would go on.

Notre Dame Fighting Irish
vs.
UCLA Bruins
Purcell Pavilion at the Joyce Center
Notre Dame, IN

Brian Kelly arrived on campus along with a light dusting of snow and a heavy media presence. My fellow diehards Dallas and Adam joined me as we biked furiously over to the football facilities to catch him just before he walked into his new office for the first time. There he was, along with our ingeniously sly athletic director Jack Swarbrick, a gaggle of gawking photographers, and a swarm of salivating reporters waiting for something—anything—they could turn into a story. I gave them some free material when I yelled out, "Welcome home, coach! Return us to glory!" He cracked a smile while telling us that he appreciated our support, then the cameras swung in my direction and the microphones jarred for space in front of my face.

I explained the significance of that moment to the reporters by likening it to the second coming of our savior. Telling them to mark my words, I predicted that Brian Kelly would go down in history as one of the greatest of all time. Then I jokingly prophesied that I would get to travel to a national championship as a student before graduating from Notre Dame Law School in three years. I had no doubt this Boston Catholic with the blood of a fighting Irishman could bring us back to the Promised Land.

☘

A few days later we revived our classic basketball rivalry against UCLA to send our students off for Christmas break on a high note. Everyone on campus came out to pack the Joyce Center and release some post-finals stress, including the first Biletnikoff Award winner in Notre Dame history, Golden Tate, and the thirty-first head coach of the Fighting Irish football team, Brian Kelly. I had already scoped out the UCLA cheerleaders at my favorite pizza place, Rocco's, the night before, even going so far as to invite them to our cheerleading-squad Christmas party later that evening right in front of their coach. They politely refused my invitation, and I waved at them sheepishly from across the court when they arrived for our game.

The highlight of our 84-73 win over the Bruins came when the new face of Fighting Irish Football made a surprise guest appearance. Brian Kelly looked as giddy as a schoolboy while he waited to take the court at halftime. Just minutes before his first public speaking engagement as the big man on campus, it dawned on me that we hadn't come up with a hand sign for the cheer our student section would perform in honor of our new head coach when the band played Tchaikovsky's *1812 Overture*. Knowing the song would accompany him onto the floor, I approached Brian with my dilemma. He passed the buck back to me by saying I should come up with something right there on the spot. We went with the "Kelly K." He laughed while we practiced it, saying, "This is what it's all about! I already love this place."

Our new leader looked right at home standing at center court while speaking to our student section. He told us to hit the weight room every day from now until the fall because we had a lot of pushups coming our way next football season. When he took on a more serious tone, I could tell he truly understood Notre Dame. Player development, recruiting the right kind of guys, hard work every day, and reviving our tradition of excellence became his talking points. According to him, success at Notre Dame meant trips to the national championship every year. Having just signed up for three more years at Notre Dame Law School, that sounded pretty good to me.

After he finished speaking, I handed my new hero his first piece of Notre Dame memorabilia: an autographed photo of myself with the words "Here's to putting the *fight* back in the Fightin' Irish" scribbled under my signature. I told him he could only keep it if he promised to read the note I wrote him. He gladly accepted both, and I went back to Buffalo for Christmas break hoping he really read my words:

> Coach Kelly,
>
> The Fighting Irish that generations of Americans grew up hearing about in tales of greatness, the Fighting Irish that represented a standard to live by for my Irish Catholics of South Buffalo and your

Irish Catholics of South Boston, and the Fighting Irish that made a name for our University with only their grit and determination to depend on are the same Fighting Irish that I know you can bring back to life.

I have no doubt that you and your staff will put the *fight* back into our football team, as well as our entire Notre Dame Family. Football is the lifeblood that drives our spirit. We lost part of it this year. We need you to bring it back in full. God speed as you go forth in service of Our Lady.

GO IRISH!

Daniel Colt Collins
Notre Dame Leprechaun

Debut as the Gold Leprechaun © Diane Santi

Prepping for Kickoff © Diane Santi

Taking a Stroll through the Endzone

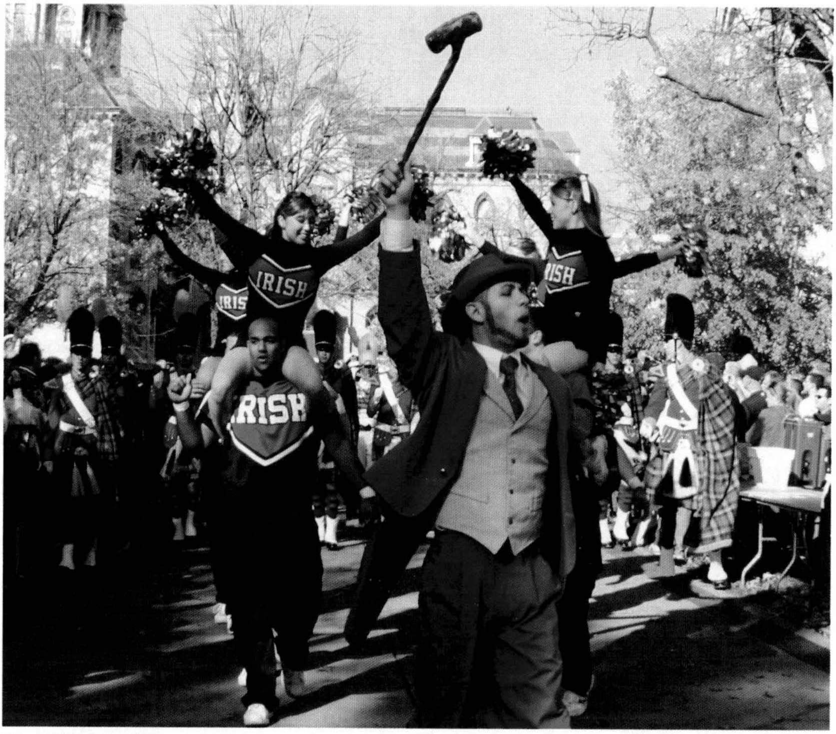

Step-Off Parade

© Diane Santi

Following my Escort

© Diane Santi

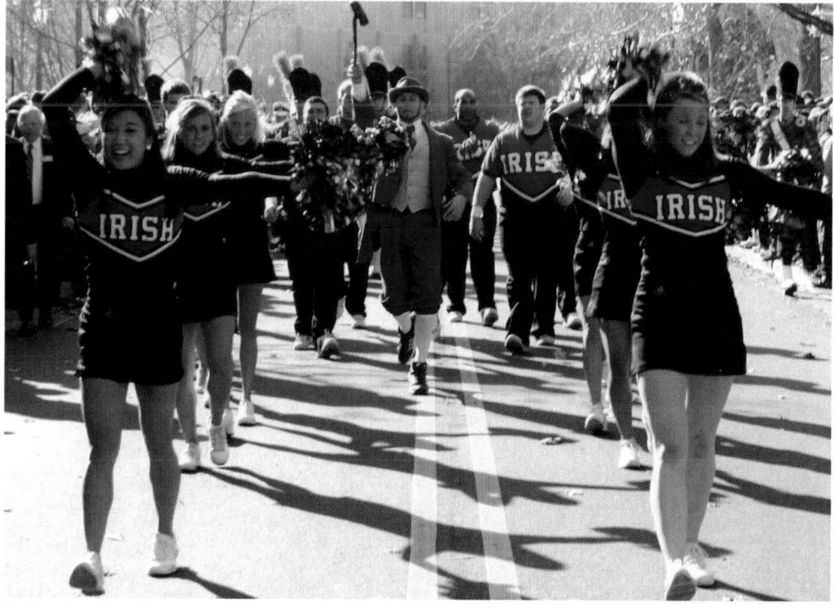

Heeere come the Irish! © Brian Egendoerfer

The Buildup to Kickoff © Brian Egendoerfer

Taking it all in © Brian Egendoerfer

Tip o' the Cap © Diane Santi

Getting the Fans on their Feet © Diane Santi

Sweat-soaked Pushups

Good Luck Golden

Rockin' the Mic

Shaking down the Thunder at the Joyce Center

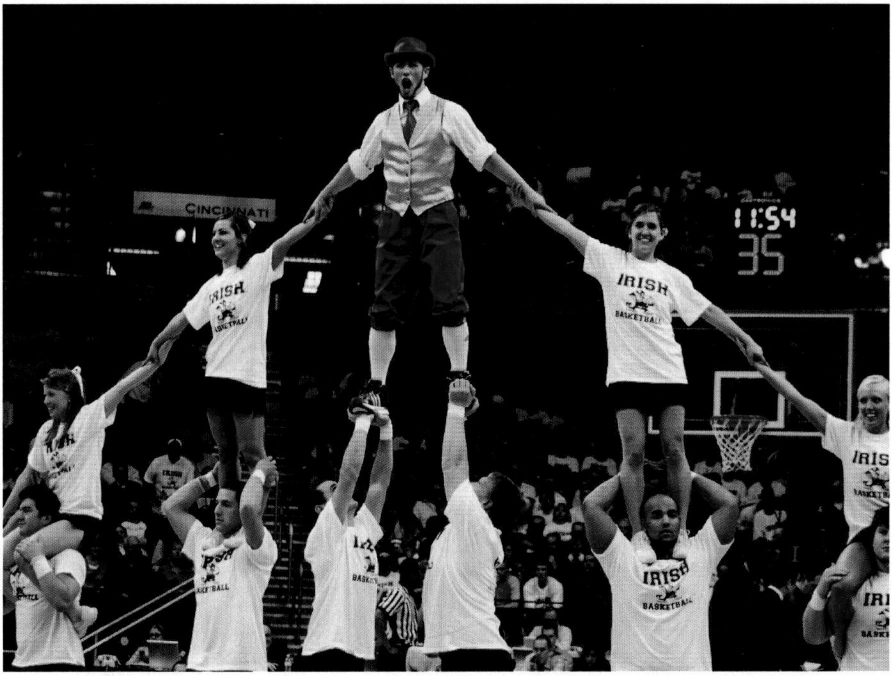

On Top of the World

© Allison Wagner Photography

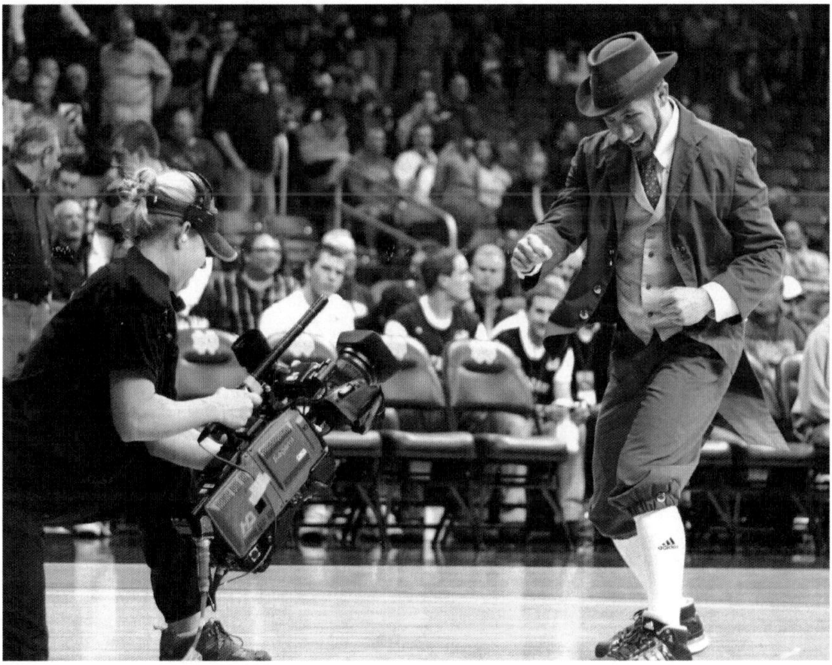

Face Time on National TV

© Allison Wagner Photography

On the Big Stage © Donald Collins

Contemplating Life with Mr. Notre Dame © Charles Cossell

Sharing Fashion Tips with Rock

Glory Days at Nichols School

© Kim Kimberly (photo courtesy of Nichols School)

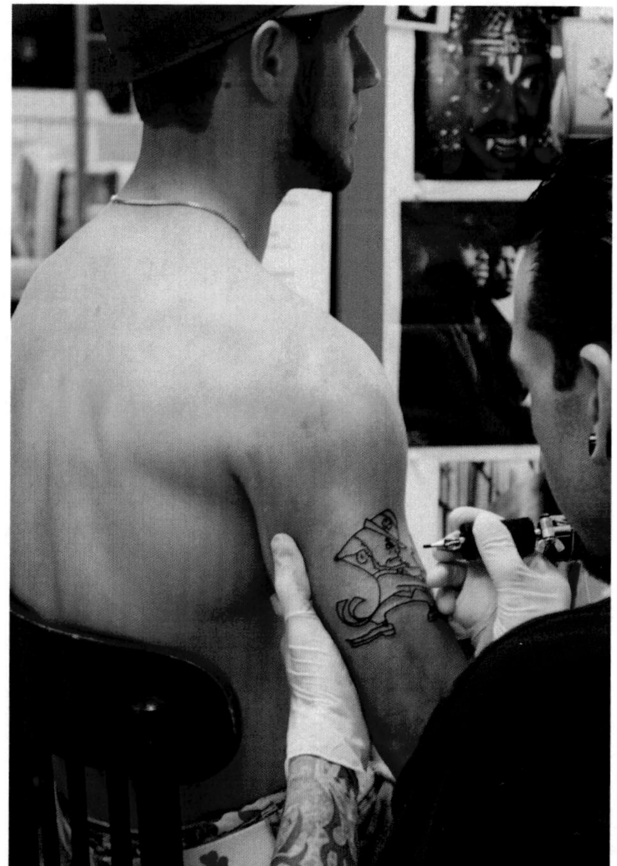

Branded for Life

Fighting Irish

In the Gold Corner...

© Allison Wagner Photography

Last appearance ever as the Leprechaun

Slap the Sign

Chapter VI

Senior Year Continued: Nothing Gold Can Stay

I RECOGNIZED THE two sophomores standing in my doorway from their usual spot in the front row at every home basketball game. They were carrying a case of Guinness so I invited them into my room. Brian Kelly had just defected from Cincinnati to join our ranks at Notre Dame, and they wanted to spread the word about t-shirts they had created to commemorate the momentous occasion in front of a national TV audience when our basketball team played his former Bearcats. As a spokesman for our student body, I had the ability to get their message out. I considered it a fair trade when I informed our classmates of the opportune time to buy their cleverly designed apparel and, in return, they left me with 24 chilled parting gifts.

The free Guinness tasted especially good as I sat with my feet up on my desk opening letters that had accumulated in my mailbox over winter break. At least three Christmas cards featured photos of me holding babies, and a few more included shots with fans from around the country. Apparently I helped families spread Christmas cheer everywhere from Palo Alto to Pittsburgh without even knowing it. One envelope with a San Antonio return address had been sent to "The Leprechaun at Notre Dame." The photo inside captured me amidst a teeming mob next to the Alamo while I knelt down with my fists raised alongside three little kids in green and gold Notre Dame football jerseys. With the card came a handwritten note:

> Dear Sir,
>
> We want to wish you a very merry Christmas and a happy New Year. Thank you for taking this picture with us. We really had fun at the pep rally in San Antonio. We don't know your address so we are sending this to Notre Dame. We really hope you get it. Go Irish!
>
> Love, Rey (age 10) Selena (age 7) and Ruben (age 6)

Blood rushed to my head and my veins hardened into heavy lead pipes. The voices on the opposite side of the table tore into me about respecting their authority, working through proper channels, and acting as a responsible representative of Notre Dame. They told me that my life wasn't a fairytale, and I should have felt grateful for their decision to suspend me indefinitely rather than fire me for good. Once I heard the word "indefinitely" my own thoughts drowned out the verbal daggers they threw at me. All noise ceased and the whole room spun as their faces grew redder and redder. I sunk into my seat, feeling dazed and confused until the lecture stopped and I snapped back into the painful reality of my suspension. Defeated, I could barely lift my eyes to meet theirs when they demanded I turn in my Leprechaun suit. I agreed to bring it in the next day, and then I slumped out the door feeling thoroughly dejected and nauseated.

I suspected a much deeper discontent behind my suspension. One controversial t-shirt couldn't have caused such a strong reaction. It probably had something to do with my consistent refusal to write out pep-rally speeches ahead of time, my edgy emcee lingo, my resistance to overly structured sideshows at the Irish Green, my love for crowd surfing and, of course, the shockingly shameful Mohawk I shaved into my head during "Beat SC Week." It all combined into one enormous firestorm when I slipped up big time by failing to fully consider the consequences of my actions. I definitely messed up, but I certainly hadn't been malicious.

Honestly, I never experienced much remorse after what happened. No one gave me the authority to take some of the actions I took, but they hadn't explicitly forbidden me to do any of it either. Working within the grey areas of their policy, I had become somewhat of a maverick mover and shaker just so I could wake up the echoes for our loyal sons and daughters. I did what I did to honor Notre Dame and to stand up for my fellow Domers. Mistakes were inevitable, but I always strove to carry out the tradition begun by Sorin and Rockne. If I had to suffer to revive the spirit of Notre Dame, then so be it. Confident in my convictions, I lived my life with no regrets.

Though I stayed firm in my beliefs, the whole sticky situation left me feeling hopelessly abandoned. Then our cheerleading captain, Kelsey, came to my rescue. She kindly offered her helping hand to assist me as I did everything possible to get reinstated. Kelsey had always been the glue that held our crazy squad together, and I loved her for the support she gave me during the most trying time of my life at Notre Dame. I vowed to take a positive life-changing lesson away from it all so I could become a better man while staying true to myself.

The first game of my suspension turned into torture as I watched from the tiny TV in my dorm room while all my friends cheered on my beloved Fighting Irish across campus in the Joyce Center. I did enjoy watching the cameras chase my teammate Steph around the court to capture as much footage as they could of her platinum blonde hair bouncing up and down to the beat of our fight song. Other than that, seeing everyone's smiling faces tormented me more than I could handle. I turned off my TV when we still had the lead, feeling guilty later on when I learned about our last-minute loss.

After just one day I couldn't take it any longer, so I asked permission to attend our games as a spectator. When the powers that be said they couldn't stop me, I began to see the light at the end of the tunnel. Joining my fellow diehards in the front row of the student section turned out to be a blast. My apprentice Leprechaun Dave did his thing, and I felt a sense of satisfaction in knowing that he would become a fan favorite once I passed the lucky shillelagh on to him.

Almost everyone who approached me about my suspension assumed it had something to do with partying. I told them that I thought such Irish stereotypes had fallen by the wayside ever since Kennedy served as our president in the 1960s. Then the probing inquiries finally ended when someone must have realized that the Curse of the Suspended Leprechaun was ruining our season. They reinstated me after three straight losses, and I brought the luck of the Irish back to our team when we dominated #12-ranked Pitt during my first game back. Now that I knew how easily I could lose it all, I made sure to fully appreciate every moment. I posed for as many photos as I could, I depleted our stock of free t-shirts by distributing them to nearly every deserving fan, and I even busted out the huge blue and gold flag usually reserved for football games.

Mike Brey's feisty team resumed its winning ways, and I wore my khakis covered in embroidered shamrocks all week long in anticipation of our senior game. Getting there early, I paid my respects to the loyal members of the Leprechaun Legion in the front row. After a few photo opps on the court, I told my Dawg Tim Abromaitis and my good friend Joey Brooks that my lucky shillelagh had the power to bring them both double-doubles that night. Always a team player, Joey carried the shillelagh around to all his teammates. Its placebo effect worked, and we came out swinging in a hard-fought 58-50 victory over Connecticut. Our scrappy point guard Tory Jackson must have been a football fan, because he made sure not to let the Huskies trample on another one of our senior games. We mobbed him after the win, and I got covered in bright blue body paint, courtesy of the crazies in our student section.

While waiting for the band to strike up our Alma Mater, the cheerleaders and I started one last "WE ARE ND!" chant. The entire Joyce Center rose up all at once to join in, and none of us could hold back our tears by the time we linked arms to sway together. The proud moment made for a fitting tribute to the place where I had formed so many of my fondest memories. Not only had the Joyce Center housed our celebration on the court after we upset Alabama when we were merely freshmen, but it had served as the site of Mike Brey's inconceivable home winning streak that somehow lasted all the way through our junior year. Most important, it had given us shelter as sophomores when we sought refuge after our early morning cold pizza and beer.

Not by coincidence, the three-game losing streak we suffered during my suspension gave way to a seven-game winning streak upon my return. Those wins included upsets over two ranked teams, as well as a thrilling overtime victory in our regular season finale at Marquette. A few of the cheerleaders and I had taken a road trip to Milwaukee so we could witness our rivalry game against the Golden Eagles in person. Due to the generosity of my family friend Lazar Hayward, who happened to be Marquette's star player, we drew the attention of the whole arena by sitting in his courtside seats. Our bright green Leprechaun Legion shirts clashed with the solid sea of gold worn by the opposing fans around us, but our kind hosts welcomed us with a sense of grace we weren't used to after our experiences during football season. They didn't even spit on us or threaten us with a sledgehammer when our stone-cold sniper, Tim Abromaitis, sent the game into overtime with a clutch, game-tying three-pointer. Then Carleton Scott ruined their senior night with a game-winning shot at the end of overtime, and we found ourselves celebrating loudly in an otherwise noiseless arena.

Our lucky day continued when Charles got pulled over for speeding just two miles away from the Notre Dame exit and the cop let him go with a warning. I joked that it paid to keep a Leprechaun in the back seat at all times. Mulligan's Bar and Grill had become our home away from home, so we stopped in to celebrate our winning streak and kick off spring break with our favorite hosts, Pat and Sue. They had packed up their whole lives to move across the country so they could open a bar as close to our campus as possible. No one bled purer shades of blue and gold. Sue nearly had a panic attack the first time she met me, and she always treated the cheerleaders like her own children. On this particular occasion, we brought them signed photos of ourselves to hang in the entrance of their bar. In return, they rewarded us with a few extra trays of little plastic cups, filled with an unknown fiery green substance.

The kindhearted staff at Mulligan's made sure that our libations kept flowing and our toasts kept rising to the Fighting Irish until closing time came. Then Pat told Charles and me to meet him out back. We hopped into his pickup truck, and he drove us to three local sacred spots where he made nightly pilgrimages—Knute Rockne's grave, the Grotto, and the cross in the woods along St. Joseph's Lake. We watched him pray reverently at all three sites, and then he dropped us off in front of the Golden Dome as the sun came up. Before we parted ways, he left us with some of the most inspiring words I had ever heard: "Now you get it. You are Notre Dame. Go make us proud."

The lucky streak my reinstatement provided for our last regular season games earned us a double-bye for the first two rounds of the Big East Tournament in New York City. That meant we had a whole lot of time, a hefty cash allowance, and a complimentary hotel room on 37th and Lex.—within walking distance of Madison Square Garden. We aptly dubbed the first half of our spring break "rock star week." Trips to Katz's Delicatessen, where they carved mouth-watering pastrami on rye, and McSorley's Old Ale House, where they preserved the classic charm of the oldest pub in New York, kept us eating, drinking, and being merry all week long. Nothing, however, could compare to our new favorite fine-dining hot spot—2 Bros. Pizza, where they served up the sloppiest, floppiest, doughy perfection we had ever tasted for only a dollar a slice. Mike, Charles, and I were in heart-attack heaven.

Conveniently, our thrifty feasting freed up most of our cash allowances for our new go-to watering hole, Third & Long, a cozy neighborhood pub with plenty of Irish Catholic pride nestled away in the heart of Manhattan. The skeptical bartender didn't believe us at first when we told her to watch for us on TV. Then we returned soon after the live broadcast of our tournament win over Seton Hall, and she poured everyone a round on the house because she felt bad for ever doubting us. We promised to buy her a round in return after we upset Pitt the next night, and she poured us one more because she liked our confidence.

The black and green shamrock tie I bought from a vendor on Canal Street must have had some Big Apple magic in it, because our team played inspired basketball as they upended #16 Pitt for the second time in just a few weeks. The win gave us another night out on the town, so we took full advantage of our freedom. The Empire State Building looked like it could light up the whole world as we bathed in its soft, looming glow from the rooftop lounge of our hotel until the dawning sun overtook its luminosity. Unfortunately, we were forced to awaken from our weeklong dream when I forgot to wear my new lucky neckwear to our semifinal game. I would have blamed myself for the loss if we all hadn't just watched West Virginia's Da'Sean Butler put on a complete clinic in front of 18,000 witnesses in the world's most famous arena. None of us wanted to leave New York, but we took consolation in knowing that our late season surge would lead to new travel plans on Selection Sunday.

☘

Whatever system they used to create the NCAA March Madness Tournament Bracket must have incorporated a sense of humor. They placed the Fighting Irish in the earliest time slot on the day after Saint Patrick's Day. I could already sense the throbbing of my imminent hangover. To make matters worse, I could see Bourbon Street from my hotel window. No 9 p.m. curfew could keep us on a leash once we realized that we had an open schedule on the one day when everyone called themselves Irish.

The Guinness began flowing at 8 a.m. while we all suited up in green from head to toe. The cheerleaders and I thought it wise to incorporate as much officially "unofficial" Notre Dame attire as possible into our outfits just to make sure everyone knew who we were. That choice turned into a bad idea immediately after our two-block trek to the French Quarter. I began to second-guess myself right away after posing for dozens of photos with fans while double-fisting pints of Guinness. Those angry voices lecturing me about protocols and authority started to sneak back into my mind, but I washed them away with shots of Jameson. After all, I still had to convert plenty of opposing fans before 9 p.m.

The Texas Longhorns pom squad committed the cardinal sin of wearing orange on Saint Patrick's Day, so I lent them some of my multiplying strings of beads and bought them a round of green beer. If only the judges from Leprechaun tryouts during my freshman year could have seen me at that moment as I extended intercollegiate diplomacy through the very drink they loathed. I patted myself on the back for a job well done when the Kentucky Wildcat mascot approached me out of costume to give me props for spreading holiday cheer so publicly.

No missed calls from authority figures awaited me the next morning, which meant that we had somehow gone undiscovered the night before, despite eventually taking over an entire balcony of the Bourbon Street Blues Company along with several members of our band. I thanked trusty ol' Saint Pat for the miracle. Making it back in time for our curfew left me feeling rather chipper around game time. I wished I could have said the same for each person stumbling and bumbling into the New Orleans Arena. Pretty much everyone in the building contributed to one big collective hangover—and it showed. Both teams played bland basketball, nearly boring the already unresponsive crowd to death. Even the officials seemed out of it by the way they made such careless calls towards the end of our eventual 51-50 loss.

I couldn't have dreamt up a worst last game ever as the Notre Dame Leprechaun, and I hoped our suffering counted as atonement for all the antics that had taken place the previous evening. Then a young woman caught my attention just before I got back onto our bus. She asked me to pose for a quick photo so she could send it to her dad who had been in the hospital for the past week. I signed my credential tag along with the words "Get well soon!" when she told me how much it would raise his spirits and hopefully bring him luck. Her eyes welled up as she thanked me, and I felt better about my last act as the Notre Dame Leprechaun.

Even after my final good deed, I had trouble getting that last horrible loss out of my head. I couldn't go out like that, not without one more win. My friends on the women's lacrosse team had a home game the next day against Syracuse, the one college I grew up hating. They didn't have to ask me twice. Not only did I watch our girls upset a team coached by the legendary lacrosse pioneer Gary Gait, but I enjoyed the perks of going back to a smaller event in a more personal venue. Tossing hot dogs into the bleachers brought back fond memories, as did sitting down next to unsuspecting kids and posing for photos with the parents of players who thanked me profusely for supporting the sport they so loved. I even got to showcase some of my own lax skills when I dusted off the stick from my high school glory days during the halftime shooting contest. My opponent, a young lacrosse junkie named David, went on to show me up with his laser-like accuracy from midfield. He embarrassed me, but I took it in stride while I soaked up the final moments before hanging my hat, retiring my shillelagh, and riding off into the sunset.

Tryout season returned to the Land of the Leprechauns, and I set to work scouring campus for my next successors. A dozen or so promising prospects joined our cheerleading practices every day for two weeks leading up to the final cuts. By then I had to compile a roster of seven worthy heirs to the throne who could deliver charming yet boisterous speeches, think on their feet at all times, fire up any given crowd, and handle every random task that happened to come their way. I already knew Leprechaun Dave was the man for the job, but I wanted to put him through the ringer just to test his wits. That left me with six more spots to fill with Leprechauns who I would feel comfortable passing my shillelagh to. In order to accomplish such an undertaking, I took our auditions to the next level by referring to everyone who tried out as my recruits, giving them a demanding pushup routine to master, and throwing as many mental tests their way as I could. Molding my minions turned into the one thing I looked forward to every day. As the first round of cuts approached, I started to feel like the host of a reality TV game show, especially when I handed each candidate a sealed envelope containing a note along with their first test:

Leprechaun Recruits,

Attached to this memo you will find a written

assessment. Fill it out. Review your answers carefully, because I don't give partial credit.

As previously stated, tomorrow you will get your first real chance to prove yourselves as the next worthy representatives of the Fighting Irish. At the end of cheerleading practice, we will exit "the pit" and you will enter one at a time to impress the cheerleaders.

You will all respond to the same situation in character as the Fighting Irish Leprechaun. Once the situation ends, our in-house talk-show host Adam will interview you briefly about the current state of Notre Dame Athletics. I suggest doing your homework so Adam doesn't make you sound like a fool.

After I watch you all in action and make my evaluations, I will post a list on the window outside Gate 3. If your name appears on that list, you will advance to the final round of tryouts. I can already tell this will be an extremely difficult decision to make, and I thank you all for giving it your best shot. You've already accomplished something special just by making it this far. I have faith that you will all continue on as great representatives of Notre Dame, whether you become the next Fighting Irish Leprechaun or not.

Now for your situation: Tomorrow marks our much-anticipated game day at the University of Spoiled Children. You must rally support for the Fighting Irish while behind enemy lines. The Notre Dame Club of Orange County and the Notre Dame Club of Los Angeles are counting on you. Grab the attention of every friendly fan in the area, but be wary of the heckling Spoiled Children scattered about. Say a few words to the crowd and generate enough energy to commence the fall of Troy.

Good luck, and GO IRISH!
LepreCollins

Leprechaun Recruit Assessment Form:

Part I: Questions (Write one sentence each.)

1. What do the words "Fighting Irish" mean to you?
2. Why did you choose to attend the University of Notre Dame?
3. What is your best memory as a student at the University of Notre Dame?

Part II: Word Association (Write the first word that comes to mind.)

1. Fr. Sorin
2. Knute Rockne
3. Clashmore Mike
4. Frank Leahy
5. Ara Parseghian
6. Lou Holtz
7. Dan Devine
8. USC
9. Green Jerseys
10. Sparty
11. Golden
12. Brian Kelly

Part III: List the three (3) most significant positions you have held as a student at the University of Notre Dame.

Part IV: In-Character Questions (Answer as the Fighting Irish Leprechaun.)

1. Favorite Color:
2. Favorite Food:
3. Favorite Sport:
4. Favorite Movie:
5. Favorite Song:
6. Favorite Class:
7. Favorite Spot on Campus:

Part V: Short Answer (Answer in one paragraph.) Why should we choose you as the next Notre Dame Leprechaun?

Part VI: Attach a picture of yourself that illustrates your love for the Fighting Irish.

Part VII: Not much here, but we need seven parts for good luck!

(Be ready to discuss your answers after Easter break.)

Once we whittled our cast of competitors down to seven, I called them all in for a top-secret briefing session. They looked startled at the sight of my newly beardless face when they arrived at our clandestine rendezvous point. I told them that I gave myself razor burn for a reason. My time was up. It was their turn to shine. They passed around the photos I had printed out of legendary, war-veteran Notre Dame alums Mario "Motts" Tonelli and Robert Patrick "Rocky" Bleier. We all shared in the legacy that such men and many more like them carried on their backs through the toughest of times. I made sure all seven of my recruits understood just how serious of a mission they would take on as representatives expected to preserve the spirit of Notre Dame. They solemnly swore to serve with honor if given the chance, and I dismissed them to prepare for their final test. As they walked out the door, I handed them one last letter:

> Leprechaun Finalists,
>
> This is it, the ultimate Fighting Irish showdown. You will each introduce one of the following Notre Dame legends as part of your game situation tomorrow:
>
> 1. Rocky Bleier
> 2. Motts Tonelli
> 3. Mike Brey
>
> Grab the mic from me and establish yourself with the crowd when you hear me call out your name. I will tell you who to introduce on the spot, so be ready. After your introduction, I will give you a game situation and let you take it away. The stage is yours. I want you to bring the swagger, confidence, and *fight* expected of a proud Fighting Irish Leprechaun. You definitely have what it takes. Don't let me down.
>
> God speed, and GO IRISH!
> LepreCollins

My gutsy understudy Leprechaun Dave proved himself as the next chosen one, and a new star was born when a little-known Minnesotan claimed the title "Clashmore Mike" in honor of our original mascot. They both had that "it" factor every Leprechaun shared. Dave could do a mean back flip, and Mike could grow chin whiskers like nobody's business. After I let them both have their "dreaded list" moments outside Gate 3, I began a new Leprechaun ritual by praying with them at the Grotto, walking around Saint Mary's Lake, and passing a bottle of Jameson around while looking up at the Golden Dome. We talked about what it meant to become the face of the Fighting Irish, and then I left them to discuss the year ahead. I felt comforted knowing that our legacy as Leprechauns rested in Dave's hands. The Jameson in my belly inspired me to write a retirement letter:

> To all my fellow Fightin' Irishmen,
>
> I want to thank you all for coming out and representing Notre Dame with pride over the past few weeks. I loved working with you all, and the passion you brought every day gave me a great way to end my career as the Leprechaun.
>
> Congratulations to Gold Leprechaun Dave and Blue Leprechaun Mike. I know they will both represent Our Lady's University honorably as they carry on the Fightin' Irish spirit with unrelenting energy.
>
> To the five others I included in this message: You all showed me something great out there, and I highly respect you for your dedication to Notre Dame. I love the fact that such vocal leaders will lead our student section at every game next year. I ask you to continue carrying that Fightin' Irish spirit with you wherever you go. Never stop inspiring all those around you.
>
> God bless, and GO IRISH!
> The artist formerly known as LepreCollins

My first day of early retirement felt strange. Hundreds of elementary school students on a tour of campus passed me by without even a single whisper or any surprised looks. It almost felt nice to walk around unnoticed, but then I saw a swarm of kids attacking Leprechaun Dave just for a chance at a photo. Envy set in like a ton of bricks. I just stood there, all alone, watching Dave make every kid's day. It took that image to make me realize how life could change in an instant, the window could slam shut rather quickly, and I could find myself already washed up at age twenty-one.

Our end-of-the-year banquet featured speeches from every senior on the cheerleading squad, along with enough tears to fill an Olympic-size swimming pool. Our captain Kelsey left us with some insightful remarks about the way our national TV appearances, autograph requests, photo shoots, and pseudo-celebrity lives had become so normal for us. She told us not to feel bad when the spotlight finally faded, but rather to reflect on the ordinary acts that had become so extraordinary through the blessed lives we lived. Reminding us that simple gestures could go a long way no matter who they came from, she asked us to carry the lessons we learned as representatives of Notre Dame with us when we went out to make the world a better place. Not even Charles could hold back his tears after that one. All of us felt connected by a force much stronger than any family tree. We knew we would remain bonded for life through the unbreakable web that pulled us together.

When my turn to give a senior speech came, I tried to provide some comic relief by listing off every rule we had broken over the past two years together. We had shared many a good time, but that wasn't what it was all about. The looks of wonderment on fans' faces, the tears in their eyes, and knowing we had contributed so greatly to how much Notre Dame meant to so many people made our jobs the best in the world. When it came down to it, we were all entertainers. That simple fact didn't belittle what we did, though. Entertainment, whether through sports, film, music, art, or giving a speech at a pep rally, gave people a chance to escape and allow themselves to get carried away by a greater power. Inspiration could spring up spontaneously whenever that happened. The seeds of that inspiration could then take root, sprout, and blossom into something amazingly beautiful. As part of that process, we all impacted the world far more than we could ever imagine. I hoped my teammates would remember that simple fact forever.

Senior week sped by in the form of a continuously slushy, sloppy, hot mess. Then commencement weekend came, along with the chaotic confusion of saying hello to family members and goodbye to best friends at the same time. Most details didn't stick, but I remembered the one piece of advice that our esteemed president emeritus, Father Theodore Hesburgh, gave at my graduation ceremony for the Kroc Institute of International Peace

Studies. He spoke of the difference between significance and success, explaining it with the simple eloquence of a Saint. According to Father Ted, striving for success in the eyes of society merely led to emptiness in the end. For that reason, success must only serve as a vehicle for attaining a higher goal. That goal was significance. Success would indeed provide for a limited number of those around us, but significance would reach far beyond what any of us could accomplish alone. Influencing others by becoming significant in their lives could empower them to become significant in turn. The whole cycle could become a chain reaction, generating inspiration and awakening hope in countless more. As it reached further and further, significance could provide the spark needed to produce a limitless light. Without boundaries, that light could allow everyone to find their own way. After he floored us with his sagacious lesson, Father Ted shook our hands and handed us our diplomas. I thanked him for giving me a goal to work towards for the rest of my life.

Chapter VII

Life after Leprechaun: Stay Golden

IT DIDN'T END. The more time that separated me from my previous life as the Leprechaun, the more I realized that it probably never would. Notre Dame had become part of my identity, as permanent as the logo inked into my arm. It followed me everywhere—from back home in Buffalo all the way to the beautiful beaches of Southern California, where I spent my summer between graduation and law school.

While in Trojan territory, I watched cheerfully as the NCAA punished our cheating rivals by erasing the loathsome "Bush Push" game from every record book. The righteous delivery of justice handed down to them called for a celebratory trip to Southern Cal, where I visited their soon-to-disappear seventh Heisman trophy. Before I left, I made sure to hide a small Irish charm somewhere near the statue of their mascot, "Traveler the Trojan Horse." Along with my miniature parting gift lay the dreaded Curse of the Leprechaun, set to bring misfortune to every Spoiled Child who passed by that spot for the rest of eternity. I couldn't wait until we met again in November, when the fates would finally turn back in our favor.

Soon after returning to Notre Dame for law school, I learned that my workload would completely crush my will to live if I let it. Not willing to sacrifice my own well-being or my loyalty to Our Lady's University, I decided to rearrange my priorities. The spirit of Notre Dame didn't come to me from within the dark recesses of the law library. It flourished out in the open where I could share it freely. Attending every pep rally, tailgating before every football game, and celebrating campus life allowed me to embrace Notre Dame without succumbing to the soul-sucking mentality of a first-year law student.

Either my steadfast devotion to Notre Dame paid off, or the curse I cast on Southern Cal worked—or both. Unfazed by the effigy of a Leprechaun hanging from a gnarly tree outside the Coliseum, I waved my "Kill So. Cal" Tricolour Irish flag with pride while watching my Fighting Irish steal back the Jeweled Shillelagh. As expected, a light drizzle and temperatures in the low sixties kept the fair weather Trojan fans from filling their own house. We took advantage by creating a student section of our own in a vast area of unoccupied seats. When my Dawg Harrison Smith sealed Southern Cal's fate with an interception on the goal line during the closing seconds, an army of security guards surrounded us to make sure we couldn't rush the field. We didn't care. Singing our fight song with full heart and voice until it echoed through the cavernous corridors of the Coliseum left us feeling perfectly content.

Returning to Alumni Hall as an assistant rector under the direction of our legendary Big Dawg Father George Rozum injected a sense of purpose into my final two years of law school. Along with my colleagues Paul "The Law" DiPietro, Michael "The Wrangler" Wrapp, and the cast of kindhearted RAs we had the honor of working with, I was able to give back to the community that had always welcomed, comforted, and inspired me from the very beginning. Father George stood as the driving force behind that community. So many generations of Dawgs owed so much to his compassionate vision. He made sure we stood above the rest when it came to building a brotherhood, and our in-house hero, Father Bill Lies, left everyone who went on the annual Dawg Retreat feeling even more connected by our common goal—serving as role models, both on campus and out in the world.

My best moments as an assistant rector came at the beginning of each year when I watched our incoming freshmen bond together through the same Dawg Run I had once struggled to complete. Father George even let me add to the tradition by giving a speech outside the tunnel of Notre Dame Stadium before they got underway. Standing next to the statue of Knute Rockne with my Leprechaun hat cocked forward on my head and a bullhorn hanging around my neck, I told my excited audience a story that blended a bit of truth into the mostly fictional folklore I had invented:

"Dawgs! This statue stands in honor of Knute Rockne, the greatest football coach of all time. No other man has given more glory to Notre Dame. Years ago I had the honor of leading our football team onto that field inside the house that Rockne built. We gave our stadium that name because Rock literally built it with the money he earned from his three national championships. Not many know that two other buildings stand on our campus because of that same collection of cash. The first didn't turn out so well, and today we call that mistake Dillon Hall.... But the second stands as a monumental shrine to all that is good in this world, forever linked with Rockne and the greatest of all those who have gone on to graduate from Notre Dame. There's a reason he wanted his image etched into its stone walls along with his beloved dog—our original mascot, Clashmore Mike. Its hallowed halls have always served as the home of our most fearless, upstanding, and classy gentlemen on campus...men who all Domers look up to. After tonight, it will serve as the place you can all call home. Welcome, gentlemen. You are now Blessed Men and Brothers of Alumni Hall. All hail the King! All hail Alumni!"

My Dawgs responded with a howling fury that I could still hear echoing through the calm nighttime air when they reached the far corners of our campus. Then I smoked a Nicaraguan cigar nice and slow on the steps of the Golden Dome until they made their way back to me. I contemplated the long shot of a chance that had first brought me to the place I now called home, and I thought about my own classmates who had become my brothers through this very same ritual. Each of them continued to write their own stories as they went out into the world to do God's work, but I knew they would all agree about the powerful effect of that first sweaty, exhausted, glorious Alma Mater.

☘

It didn't take too long before I diagnosed myself with a severe case of Leprechaun nostalgia. Leprechaun Dave got to make a guest appearance on the "Live with Regis and Kelly" show, Clashmore Mike starred in a SportsCenter Commercial, and the next man in line, Leprechaun Bryce, kicked off our 2012 football season with a weeklong trip to Ireland. Trying to live vicariously through my rock-star successors turned me so green with envy that my skin matched the retired Leprechaun hat hanging on my wall. I needed a diversion. Joining the Notre Dame boxing team provided that and so much more.

Knute Rockne founded our boxing program in 1920. After his tragic death, the tradition he started went on to embody the spirit of Notre Dame itself. Under the direction of boxing guru Dominic "Nappy" Napolitano, we became the pinnacle of amateur collegiate fighting while at the same time staying committed to honor, strength, and service. For over 80 years, every dollar raised at our annual "Bengal Bouts" tournament funded medical facilities and an entire school system run by the Congregation of Holy Cross Missions in Bangladesh. Several of my Dawgs had contributed greatly to the cause by becoming award-winning boxers. My friend Mike Lee even went on to become a professional prizefighter. The tattoo on my right arm had been waiting with its fists raised for far too long. I had to give it a shot.

No other sport ever brought me closer to the edge physically or mentally, and the principle behind it all pushed me even further. Boxing forced me to break through every self-created barrier to become a better man. Bengal Bouts had an added feel of purity about it that captured my soul. I shared everything with my fellow fighters, from backbreaking workouts to a sense of significance. We all knew exactly what our teammates had gone through to get there. After months and months of training together, we gained the ultimate level of respect for each other. Then we squared off in the ring.

I thought that stepping between the ropes onto that raised canvas platform with photographers and fans surrounding me would feel a lot like the rush I got every time I led our football team out of the tunnel into Notre Dame Stadium. I was wrong. Nothing compared to the unrestricted surge of electricity running through my veins before each fight. My nerves spiked every time I put on that golden robe and a Holy Cross priest blessed me prior to my march into the ring. Once I got to that point, it was no longer about my opponent. It was about facing up to my own fears and forgetting my own limitations. With every single insecurity on display and no one else in the ring to lean on, I had to overcome myself completely. It wasn't a matter of choice. It was a matter of survival.

The second that bell rang, everything else went away. I had chosen Colt "Pony Boy" Collins as my fight name. My trainer, Father Brian Daley, and my corner man, Brett "The Dough Boy" Geschke, both yelled out, "Stay golden!" as I advanced towards my first opponent. That was the last thing I heard before the bell rang again and I sat down on the rusty old stool in my corner, already covered in blood. They told me it wasn't my blood. That was a good sign. I didn't let up until I won by a TKO in the second round. Advancing to the quarterfinals, I won my next fight before it even began when I stared down my opponent and he flinched. After taking him to the ropes for three straight rounds, I went on to the semifinals. My lanky adversary Mark Frego and I both knew what was about to go down when we touched gloves out of respect to begin our bout. The next six minutes encompassed an all-out war of wills, leaving both of us unable to lift our arms when the final bell rang. I lost by split decision, but I tasted triumph. Anyone could have walked into that ring, but I learned a lesson that could only come from feeling my own mouth fill up with blood and moving forward anyway.

In his third year as our head coach, Brian Kelly did indeed lead us to the Promised Land as I had so boldly predicted upon his first arrival. I pretended to have known all along, but no one could have anticipated the 2012 undefeated season that seemingly came out of nowhere. We all should have recognized the Irish Tricolour flag cleats our team wore for their season opener in Ireland as a good omen. After dominating Navy in the Emerald Isle Classic on the Old Sod, close calls against Purdon't and the Skunkbears kept us on edge. Taking care of business against Miami during the recently renewed Catholics versus Convicts rivalry in our adopted hometown of Chicago gave us a boost, but doubts still lingered about the real identity of our team. Everyone finally felt the magic when our defense made a goal-line stand for the ages against Stanford. The Fighting Irish Faithful literally shook the foundation of Notre Dame Stadium with the volley cheer they sent on high. Anyone questioning whether the echoes had really awakened left that game with little doubt.

With our record standing at 6-0, everyone expected us to capture our lucky seventh win without any real problems against BYU. A group of alums from the class of 1970 and their families chose that game to make their annual pilgrimage to Knute Rockne's grave. They asked me to say a few words about Rock, and I eagerly accepted their somewhat secretive invitation when they told me to arrive at the cemetery gates at 9:30 a.m. on game day. I returned to my favorite sacred site ready to give a speech that I hoped might make Rock smile down on us for the rest of our resurgent season. Then my hosts raised shots of Jameson around his plot, and I knew I had come to the right place. We even left one on his headstone so he could celebrate the win later that afternoon. I read the words I had written out the night before, hoping they would lend some extra significance to the priceless scene I had just witnessed:

To my fellow alums, current students, and all members of our Notre Dame Family: Thank you for including me in this remarkable tradition.

We hear the word "tradition" a lot on our campus, many times alongside pleas to preserve traditions or uphold traditional standards. In 1923, Knute Rockne shocked and outraged Notre Dame traditionalists by garbing his team in bright green jerseys rather than their traditional blues for their game against then-powerhouse Princeton. Not only did it work as an ingenious motivational ploy, but it served to give his quarterbacks easier targets for the state-of-the-art forward pass offense he had invented. In response to the criticism he received from the traditionalists who questioned his ways, Rock stated with conviction that, whenever college tradition interfered with college football strategy, he would gladly give up the so-called tradition.

For a man who represents the origin of many a proud tradition here at Notre Dame, that single thought speaks volumes. When I think of Rock, I think of those words and I think of a fearless innovator who seized every opportunity without fearing change. Most important, I think of a Notre Dame Man who found ways to keep moving forward while staying true to his own personal set of standards.

As I stand here with all of you in remembrance of Rock, I think the best way to honor him and the rich legacy he left behind is to carry on in his tradition of embracing uncertainty while upholding the standard of excellence that makes Notre Dame rise above the rest. God bless, and go Irish!

I thanked God for giving me the chance to start my day by honoring the greatest football mind of all time when our team needed a miracle to beat BYU. Then I thanked Our Lady for listening to the Hail Marys I repeated every time it looked like we were dead in the water against Pitt. Three overtimes later, we somehow pulled off our ninth win of the season. Despite our lack of style points, our winning ways continued until we found ourselves in a showdown against our Trojan rivals for a shot at the national championship. Southern Cal had started the season ranked #1 while we flew under the radar unranked. The Curse of the Leprechaun must have remained intact, because the tables had turned by the time we marched into the Coliseum as the top team in the nation to face our already-eliminated inferior opponents. Not even the most imaginative sports writers could have made this stuff up. My lucky seventh year as a student concluded with a 22-13 win when our intrepid running back Theo Riddick made a mockery of the Trojan defense. I brandished my "Kill So. Cal" Irish Tricolour flag blatantly for all to see as we filled those corridors with echoes of our fight song once again.

"We're going to South Beach" had already become the quote of the year when every Domer I ever met flocked to Southern Florida to start 2013 in style. Notre Dame had finally made it back to the big show, and the Fighting Irish Faithful let everyone else know exactly how they felt about it. While hound's-tooth-wearing Alabama fans strolled around Miami with a blasé "been there, done that" attitude, we showed the nation what a real fan base should look like. No inch of soft white sand remained uncovered when tens of thousands watched our pep rally along the Atlantic coastline. No opportunity to show support went by without thousands more showing up in blue, gold, and green. Most important, no Alabama fans won any rap battles or dance-offs at The Clevelander—thanks to my Dawgs Charles and Trey.

Sean O'Rourke had long since earned his stripes as a Notre Dame diehard, but he laid claim to his rightful spot on the throne as the Tailgating King of the World in the parking lot of Sun Life Stadium on January 7, 2013. My friend Brian drove his RV up from the Florida Keys, and $800 later we had it stuffed to the gills with 30 cases of beer, a full bar, burgers, brats, hot dogs, chips, salsa, guac, foldable lawn chairs, and enough ice to sink the *Titanic*. Two separate news crews stopped by to interview us about our setup, which included a big-screen satellite TV that we used to watch ourselves later in the afternoon. A somewhat suspect lottery system had left most of us ticketless, but we put on a national-championship-caliber party anyway.

Robert Buynak, who graduated from Notre Dame in 1991, reminded me of the bond that unites every member of the Notre Dame Family when, twenty-two years later, he offered me his extra ticket to the biggest game since my birth. He happily joined our tailgate with his kids, who watched my friends and me make our Alma Mater proud by flawlessly executing the largest group beer shotgun any of us had ever seen. We knew our Fighting Irish would win when we spiked our cans of Coors against the pavement without wasting a single drop. Our time had finally come!

☘

I knew Alabama had us beat when they went up 14-0 after only their second possession of the game. Our top-ranked defense had given up only two rushing touchdowns all year long, but an absolute beast of a running back named Eddie Lacy made us look small, slow, and weak. With our offense sputtering and our defense unable to keep up, I tried in vain to swallow the lump growing in my throat. Once again, we were so close yet so far away. Ready to concede the crown and crawl back under a rock, I contemplated leaving at halftime. In an effort to save myself from committing such a ghastly sin, I cleared my mind by taking a hike around the entire stadium. As painful as it was, I couldn't walk out on my Fighting Irish. I returned from my contemplative stroll just in time to take my seat for the opening play of the second half.

God rewarded me for confirming my loyalty to Our Lady's favorite football team. I hadn't noticed the five-year-old boy in a Manti Te'o jersey sitting directly behind me during the first half. He stayed quiet the whole time, probably experiencing the same state of shock as Charles and I. Then he grabbed my attention by turning to his dad midway through the third quarter to say, "Come on, Irish! We got this!" Alabama had already put the game well out of reach with a 35-0 lead, but this little Fighting Irish fan refused to let that deflate his optimism. He repeated the same words with a shout as if our boys in blue and gold could hear him on the field.

"Come on, Irish! We got this!" I thought about his words for a while, eventually coming to the conclusion that I agreed wholeheartedly with his simple sentiment. Then I noticed my eyes leaking like a sieve. I couldn't remember when all the losses, frustrations, and seemingly negative experiences in my life had left me so fed-up and jaded. Though it escaped my memory, there *had* to have been a time before I learned to give up hope whenever the score seemed insurmountable. I wondered what had happened to that unspoiled version of me as I twisted around in my seat to give the kid a fist bump. Without even thinking about the words leaving my lips, I said, "Get ready for some pushups next time we score." Sure enough, we crossed that goal line for the first time a few plays later and everyone around us joined in my new hero's pure joy as we tossed him laughing into the air seven times. His dad stopped me after our 42-14 loss to thank me for giving his son a memory he would always cherish. As we departed, I thanked my five-year-old friend for teaching me something so significant. He left me with an all-knowing smile and one last "Go Irish!"